Business Communication: The Basics

Olkaos
PUBLISHING

Business Communication: The Basics

Olutayo K. Osunsan

Olkaos
PUBLISHING

PUBLISHING

olkaos@gmail.com

Olkaos Publishing
P.O. Box 5788,
Kampala,
Uganda.

ISBN-13: 978-1500463878
ISBN-10: 1500463876

Contents

Preface

The Purpose of *Business Communication: The Basics* is to encourage managers and students of business management to understand the significant role of communication in life and in management. To achieve this I have attempted to combine rigor with simplicity and relevance.

The approach is direct and enables easy reading to stimulate the desire to know more about communication and the dynamics it inculcates in business.

Like most books of this nature, little in new since ideas, theories and evidence of scholars in business communication and management have been utilized. This book is distinct, however in its approach of packaging business communication in a simple and applicable manner that can be immensely useful to both students and professionals.

My gratitude goes out to all those who have used this book in its original form as a module and provided me with feedbacks and ideas. As I continue to learn, I look forward to sharing that learning with you.

Olutayo K. Osunsan
Kampala, Uganda
August 2014

Communication: the most vital skill in management and life

"I speak to everyone in the same way, whether he is the garbage man or the president of the university"
-Albert Einstein

"The way we communicate with others and with ourselves ultimately determines the quality of our lives"
-Anthony Robbins

Communication

Communication is simply defined as the act of exchanging information. It is the sharing of information between two or more individuals, groups or entities to establish a common understanding. It can be used to inform, command, assess, instruct, influence and persuade. Effective communication is defined as "the imparting or interchange of thoughts, opinions, or information by speech, writing, or signs".

Communication skills are vital in all aspects of life including business. Effective communication between individuals, especially in an organization is important in achieving the organizational objectives and results to managing people effectively. In the words of Stephen Covey, author of 'the Seven Habits of highly effective people': "communication is the most important skill in life. We spend most of our working hours communicating". Covey defines communication as "mutual understanding"

When applying for a job, your skill, knowledge and qualification are important, but equally important are your communication skills, both written and oral. This is why many employees include essay-type question in the application process in order to evaluating the communication skills. Employers place a lot of emphasis on communication skills because it will reflect on their company, the way you (the employee) communicate. Without the ability to communicate, talented, intelligent and knowledgeable people will always be doubted basing on their poor communication skills. This means even the company you work with will be doubted as well for employing a poor communicator.

By successfully getting your message across, you convey your thoughts and ideas effectively. When not successful, the thoughts and ideas that you convey do not necessarily reflect your own, causing a communication breakdowns and creating roadblocks that stand in the way of your goals – both personally and professionally.

In a survey of recruiters from companies with more than 50,000 employees, communication skills were cited as the single most important decisive factor in choosing managers. In the study conducted by the University of Pittsburgh's Katz Business School, it was also revealed that verbal and written communication skills, in addition to the ability to work with others, are the major factors contributing to job success.

In spite of the increasing importance placed on communication skills, many individuals continue to struggle with it, unable to communicate their thoughts and ideas effectively – whether in verbal or written format. This inability makes it nearly impossible for them to compete effectively in the workplace, and stands in the way of career progress. Getting your message across is paramount to progressing in business. To do this, you must understand what your message is, what audience you are sending it to, and how it will be perceived. You must also weigh-in the circumstances surrounding your communications, such as situational and cultural context.

Characteristics of Communication

Communication takes place when one person transfers some understandable information to another person. It also includes the transmission of thoughts, opinions, feelings, facts, and information between two or more persons. Several characteristics describe the dynamic nature of communication, some of which include:

1. Communication is unavoidable – We are always communicating; verbally on nonverbally, through our dress code, our presence or absence, what we do or don't do, etc.
2. Communication operates at two levels – Every communication consists of two aspects, the message and the emotion.
3. Communication is irreversible – Once a message is communicated it cannot be retrieved, erased or taken back.
4. Communication is a process – Communication is not an isolated event, it is a process that requires time and procedures to achieved effective communication.
5. Communication is not a panacea – Effective communication can mitigate many things, but it is by no means a universal solution to all problems.
6. Communication often presents ethical challenges – Communications always have ethical implications or dilemmas, especially in the context of business.

International communication

With more and more companies globalizing, employees in various international locations now have day-to-day communications with each other, international communication, also known as cross cultural communication is inevitable. Given different cultural contexts, this brings new communication challenges to the workplace.

Even when employees speak the same language (for instance, correspondences between English-speakers in the U.S. and English-speakers in the UK), there are some cultural differences that should be considered in an effort to optimize communications between the two parties.

In such cases, effective communication strategy begins with the understanding that the sender of the message and the receiver of the message are from different cultures and backgrounds. This introduces a certain amount of uncertainty, making communications even more complex.

Without getting into cultures and sub-cultures, it is perhaps most important to realize that a basic understanding of cultural diversity is the key to effective cross-cultural communications.

Without intently studying the individual cultures and languages, we must all learn how to better communicate with individuals and groups whose first language, or language of choice, does not match our own.

Learning the basics about culture and at least something about the language of communication in the host country are necessary. This is necessary even for the basic level of understanding required to engage in appropriate greetings and physical contact, which can be a tricky area inter-culturally. For instance, kissing a business associate is considered an inappropriate business practice in the U.S, but in Paris, one peck on each cheek is an acceptable greeting. The handshake that is widely accepted in the U.S. is not recognized in all other cultures.

While many companies now offer training in the different cultures where the company conducts business, it is important that employees being thrust into communicating across cultures practice patience and work on their own to increase their knowledge and understanding of the different culture. This requires the ability to see that a person's own behaviors and reactions are oftentimes culturally driven and not intended to offend or irritate. Other things to remember when communication across cultures and national boundaries include: time zone, holidays, measurements and currency, they do vary from country to country.

Merely showing a genuine interest, paired with patience and understanding, is the best answer to communicating cross-culturally.

Importance of Effective Communication within organizations

Effective communication has always been important in business. This importance is highlighted more recently, due to the dynamic changes in the business world and the grave consequences of failed communication in contemporary business. It is now a common fact that effective communication is both an asset and a core competence to the organizations that possess them. In today's world, business people and their organizations are faced with the following changes that highlight the importance and need for effective communication:

1. **Motivates employees–** Effective communication helps communicate to employees that they are integral part of the

business. It helps to let employees know that their ideas, views and opinions matter.

2. **Effective control and coordinate business activity–** Effective communication ensures good management and coordination of the business. It helps to ensure that the right objectives are achieved within the allocated period. It enables the business to work as one entity.

3. **Successful decision making–** Effective communications makes accurate and timely information available to the decision maker which facilitates effective decision-making.

4. **Better communication with customers-** This will enable the development of right products and services that meet customer needs. Thus increasing customer loyalty which in the long run will increase sales and businesses longevity.

5. **Improve relationships with suppliers–** Effective communication enables the creation of a healthy mutually beneficial relationship between the businesses and its suppliers. This can result in better bargaining power, quality inputs, credit facilities and preferential treatment.

6. **Improves chances of obtaining finance–** Effective communication creates a strong sense of confidence among investors,

share holders and banks. This provides more willing sources for financing for the business in the case of expansions or financial difficulties.

7. **Good public relations**- Effective communication helps to create a good image for the business in the general public. The good image benefits the business in several ways.

The increase in use of technology by businesses and consumers, increased global competition, high ethical standards, need for continuous innovation and emphasis on quality have all highlight the need for effective communication. Poor communication or miscommunication by a business can lead to global negative publicity; drop in profits and all-round decline in their activities. Angry customers can twit (on twitter), post on facebook or other internet media to communication the disappointment to millions of people in minutes. This information can reach the government, banks, shareholders, suppliers and other customers.

Impact of technology on Communication in organizations

A few decades ago, the standard equipments used to conduct business included typewriters, telephones, photocopy machines and calculators. Technology has ushered in the e-mail, voice mail, teleconferencing, videoconferencing, computer networks and the internet, to mention a few; all these technologies have expanded the methods of communication. New technology has made communication even more accessible and at the same time, more complex. Technology has facilitated increased vertical and horizontal communication within the organization to encourage group problem solving, consensus building, global group projects and the overall synchronization of even global organizations (multinationals). Now companies equipped with computerized information processing systems, which include personal computers, computer networks and electronic mail systems have direct and easy access to their clients and the consumer behavior. Working out of the office is also facilitated by laptops, tablets, smart phones, cloud computing and virtual offices to mention a few.

Though change is a good thing in management, not all changes are good; hence the benefits of improved communications technology comes along with some negative aspects as well. These negative effects can come in the form of:

1. The loss of personal touch due to the adoption of internet technology such as chat rooms, Skype and other softwares.
2. Installation of monitoring software in the workplace, that indicates that employers do not trust employees.
3. Working 24 hours a day due to excessive accessibility to communication technology, which can have a negative effect on work life balance.
4. The change, upgrade and evolution of communication technology and technology generally can be very confusing for employees and clients alike. This can lead to mistakes and loss of business due to systems glitches and failures.
5. Technology has open new channels that can be used to commit crimes and defraud the organizations. These new channels may be hard to monitor and manage.

Understanding communication in management

"Developing excellent communication skills is absolutely essential to effective leadership. The leader must be able to share knowledge and ideas to transmit a sense of urgency and enthusiasm to others. If a leader can't get a message across clearly and motivate others to act on it, then having a message doesn't even matter."
-Gilbert Amelio

"Communication - the human connection - is the key to personal and career success."
-Paul J. Meyer

The communication Process

Communication is a process that involves the transmission of meaningful information from on party to another through the use of shared symbols. Communication is considered successful when the meaning is understood. The communication process model illustrates communication between two people, but can also apply to more complex communication situations. The communication process using the communication model consists of two main phases: the transmission phase (from sender) where the information is shared between two or more individual and the feedback phase (from receiver) where a common understanding is reached.

Communication barriers can pop-up at every stage of the communication process (which consists of sender, message, channel, receiver, feedback and context - see the diagrams of the models) and have the potential to create misunderstanding and confusion. A message is successful only when both the sender and the receiver perceive it in the same way.

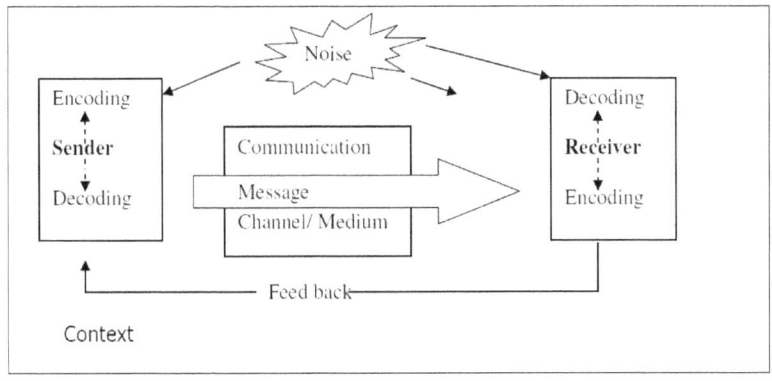

(the model below is also acceptable)

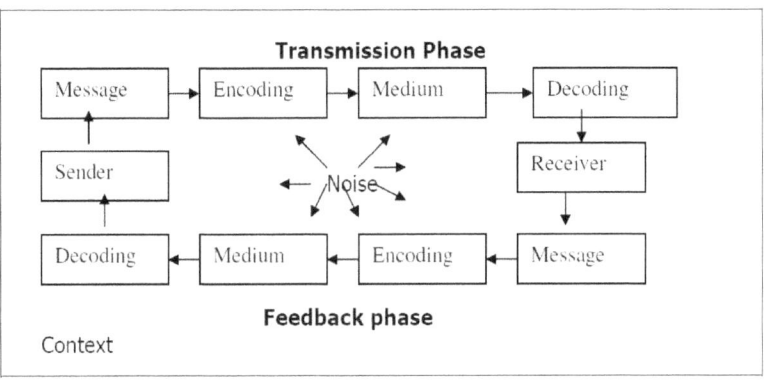

Communication begins with a sender who has a message (or information) for the receiver. The sender encodes the message and selects a communication channel (or medium) that will successfully deliver the message to the receiver.

Sender -This is the person who initiates the communication. The sender's nonverbal cues will influence the message in the perception of the receiver. To establish yourself as an effective communicator, you must first establish credibility. Physical appearance, position, knowledge, etc can all contribute to the development of credibility. More specifically, in the business arena, this involves displaying knowledge of the subject, the audience and the context in which the message is delivered. Failure to understand who you are communicating to will result in delivering messages that are misunderstood.

Message -This is the information being transmitted by the sender to the receiver, which can be spoken, written, drawn, etc. As a sender, consider the message itself. Written, oral and nonverbal communications are affected by the sender's tone, method of message organization, validity of the argument, what is communicated and what is left out, as well as your individual style of communicating. Messages also have intellectual and emotional components, with intellect allowing the ability to reason and emotion allowing presentation of motivational appeals, ultimately changing minds and actions.

Receiver -This is the individual or audience the message is intended for. As the communicator, there is no doubt you have in mind the actions or reactions you hope your message will prompt from the audience. Keep in mind, your audience also enters into the communication process with ideas and feelings that will undoubtedly influence their understanding of your message and their response to it. To be a successful communicator, you should consider these before delivering your message and acting appropriately.

Feedback -This is the response of the receiver in reaction to the message from the sender; it can be verbal or nonverbal. Your audience will provide you with feedback, verbal and nonverbal reactions to your communicated message, it is important to pay close attention to these feedbacks as they are crucial to ensuring the audience understands your message.

Context -Context is the situation in which the message is delivered. This may include the surrounding environment or broader culture (i.e. corporate culture, international cultures, a wedding, boardroom, et cetera.).

Encoding -This is the process of selecting the appropriate symbols such as written words, numbers, and digital symbols such as written words, numbers, digital symbols, sounds or body language that can be rightly decoded by the receiver. This means that the sender must consider the decoding skills of the receiver when encoding for the communication to be successful.

Communication channel -The channel is the means by which the message is delivered and it will determine the quantity and quality of information that is conveyed to the receiver. Communication channels include face-to-face conversations, group meetings, memos, policy manuals, e-mail, voice mail, videotapes, computer printouts, phone calls, TV, etc. The time availability, message complexity, size and proximity of the audience and skills of the sender will all determine the more suitable channel to us.

Decoding -This is the translation of the symbolic, verbal, written or visual symbols into an undistorted and clear message. For communication to be successful and effective, the receiver must be able to decode the message and understand its true meaning. Misinterpretations occur when the receiver is unable to decode the message due to lack of necessary language skill, culture, jargon, etc.

Noise -Another hindrance to effective communication is noise; noise can be anything that interferes with the sending and receiving of the message. Sources of noise includes the senders accent, slow internet connection, poor vision to read, limited time pressure which leads to poor listening, etc. The larger and complex an organization the more likelihood of noise need to identify communication barriers and how they can be overcome in an organization.

Due to the possibility of miscommunication, it is important that effective communication should always include opportunities for feedbacks from the receiver. The feedback enables the sender clarity the message if it has been misunderstood. Communication channels that provide for feedbacks are called two-way communications and channels that do not are one-way communications.

Communication Channels
When dealing with barriers to communication, one of the most influential determinants of effective communication is the communication channel or medium, it determines the richness of the information being communicated. Richness is the amount of information a channel or medium can carry and how effective it will be in facilitating a common understanding between the sender and the receiver. Channels with high information richness are able to carry a lot of information and ensure a common understanding between the two parties even when the information is complex. The figure below helps to clarify the explanation:

High Information Richness Channel			*Low Information Richness Channel*
-Physical presence (face to face) -Best for non routine, ambiguous, difficult messages	-Interactive channels (Telephone, electronic media)	-Personal static channel (Memos, letters, report tailored for receiver)	-Impersonal static channels (fliers, bulleting, general reports) -Best for routine, clear, simple messages

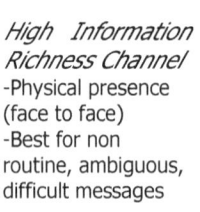

Barrier to effective communication
To be an effective communicator and to get your point across without misunderstanding and confusion, your goal should be to lessen the frequency of the barriers at each stage of

this communication process with clear, concise, accurate, well-planned communications.

Barriers to effective communication can include physical distractions, emotional distractions, cultural and language differences on a general note. More specifically, the accurate transmission of information can be disrupted by communication barriers such as the following amongst others:

1. **Perception** – No two individuals can perceive the same message in exactly the same way; people normally perceive things in a manner consistent to their beliefs, experiences, culture and general upbringing. People also tend to perceive selectively; by selecting out of the message what they want to hear and ignoring what they don't want to hear (examples: selective perception, bias and stereotyping).

2. **Semantics** – Words have different meanings to different people from various parts of the world and cultures. Semantics is the meanings of words and can be the cause of miscommunication or hindrance to effective communication (Example: "that car is 'hot'").

3. **Conflicting verbal and non-verbal communication** – People pick up signals and messages on what is being said not only by words but also from non-verbal communication, such as facial expression, bodily posture, speaking volume, etc. Conflicting verbal and non-verbal communication creates confusion due to the fact that the receiver will not be sure on which of the two messages should be taken seriously.

4. **Defensiveness** – information that clashes with a person's credibility and integrity can lead to defensive reactions, this is due to the fact that the person will not want to contribute anymore because of the fear of farther dampening his/her image. In some cases most of the communication will be spent of trying to vindicate self and not on the issue at hand.

5. **Distortion** – in the process of relaying a message from person to person in the organization the message is filtered, summarized, added on to and in the process distorted by the time it gets to the intended recipient.

6. **Rumors and the grapevine** – These are fast moving messages that move through informal groups in the organization. They

tend to be mostly false and are the result of communication gaps between the management and staff of the organization, they lead to communication being distorted and mistrusted.

7. **Narrow view point** – Some people have a tendency to focus on their areas of specialization in the organization and undermine others (from different departments, branches, sections, etc) this has a negative impact on resource allocation and hinders effective communication.

8. **Status** – Positions in the organization can also be a barrier to effective communication, the difference in rank translates to communication breakdown due to the fact that subordinates are intimidated by the image and position that a superior holds and in some cases where communication of bad news is required they will prefer not to relay the bad news to the boss. Some bosses also have a habit of forgetting subordinates and isolating themselves instead.

9. **Structural Restrictions** – The organizational chart can hinder the communication process due to formally sanctioned routes, procedures and

protocols. This means messages have to travel through the ranks and the sender has to go through long bureaucratic processes, which most employees don't have the patience or the time for.

10. **Diversity issues** – When people from different backgrounds, cultures, countries and groups work together, there is a high level of diversity which means even simple non verbal behaviors can have conflicting meanings, not to mention the verbal aspects. All this impede effective communication when not managed properly.

11. **Jargons** – The use of technical terminologies when communicating with someone who is unfamiliar field or profession is definitely a barrier to effective communication.

12. **Lack of trust, ambiguity, information overload, information under load, emotions, etc**

In today's fast changing world, cross–cultural communication is a fact of business life. One way to learn how to deal with cross-cultural communication barriers is to learn from other peoples experiences. Managers must communicate with others to enable them perform their various roles and tasks. Managers spend most of their time communicating in meetings, on phone, e-mail or face-to-face; it is estimated that more than 85% of the manager's time is spent engaging in communication; this highlights the importance of effective communication. When communication is ineffective the organization's performance suffers, competitive advantage can be lost and in some cases poor communication can be dangerous enough to lead to the tragic and unnecessary loss of human life.

Overcoming/managing Barriers to Effective communication

There will always be communication barriers due to human errors, technology failure, etc, but it has to be managed and if possible completely eradicated. To deliver your messages effectively, you must commit to breaking down the barriers that exist at each of the stages of the communication process (refer to communication model). If your message is too lengthy, disorganized, or contains errors, you can expect the message to be misunderstood and misinterpreted. The use of poor verbal and body language can also confuse the message. It is best to be mindful of the demands on other people's time, especially in today's ultra-busy society. The difference between effective and ineffective communication can be traced to how well the communicating parties deal with these other elements:

1. **Use of feedback** – The feedback helps the sender check whether the message has been accurately received by the receiver by deducing from his/her response.

2. **Simplified language** – The use of simple understandable language that can be understood by the receiver will facilitate effective communications; this excludes the use of foreign, flashy accents, sophisticated words or jargons.

3. **Active listening** – The receiver should pay close attention to the message in its fullness without interrupting or giving premature judgment. The same applies to the sender when feedback is sent.

4. **Restraining Emotions** – Both parties should recognize when emotions are running high and try to tame and control it in order to avoid its effect from hindering the communication.

5. **Matching verbal and non-verbal communication** – It is obvious that actions speak louder than words therefore it is important that both actions and words convey the same message in order to make the communication more effective.

6. **Build Trust** – An atmosphere of trust must be cultivated in the organization to overpower rumors and the grapevine. This will make every communication trust worthy and effective.

7. **Avoid triggering defensiveness** – Criticizing, arguing and even giving advice can trigger some listener's defensiveness because they want to protect their self image. The best thing is not to react immediately and action should be delayed for a convenient time depending on the person.

8. **Clarify ideas before communicating** – The planning of the message and choice of the right communication channel will make communication effective and reduce confusion.

Communication for Managers

It is a fact that communication skills are an integral workplace skill for any person who hopes to succeed in an organization. These communication skills more specifically include:

- Negotiating, bargaining, persuading and debating issues without being obnoxious or offensive to others.
- Greeting people, representing the organization in public, selling, and demonstrating products or services.
- Courteous telephone skills in both formal and informal situations.
- Reporting, transmission information, articulate in explaining issues or procedures in an understandable manner.
- Listening effectively.
- Interviewing people, drawing out others' views and ideas from others, and probing for information.
- Eloquently displaying skills in the use of language, grammar and punctuation.
- Expressing ideas in written form, editing, reviewing and preparing concise and logically written materials for various audiences.
- Developing, organizing and presenting ideas successfully for both formal and spontaneous speeches.
- Constructively leading and participating in group discussions.

Communication skills are very relevant for the progression of a manager's career. Most of a manager's time is spent communicating. Managers need to develop their communication skills to offer direction to their staff and must work with stakeholders in solving business issues. Excellent communication skills are vital for good performance management. More specific to managers are the additional ability to:

1. Convey the vision, goals and objectives of the organization with conviction strong enough to inspire the employees to buy into it.
2. Construct relationships based on trust and respect that will encourage the employees to know that they are part of a formidable team that is led by a great person.
3. Give feedback on how well and poor a task was achieved and how employees can do even better in the future.
4. Recognize the unique and distinct contribution and achievement of each and every employee.
5. Actively listen to the opinions, ideas, objection and views of employ, with the view of truly adopting valid ideas.

Human relations skills

It is important now, more than ever that people develop human relations skills (also known as interpersonal skills). This is due to the fact that the average human speaks about 18,000 words a day to individuals or groups, these words can build or destroy human relations. In business, these words can make or break the business. Interpersonal skills involve the ability to comprehend and deal with people in a productive and constructive manner that generates benevolence and helps to maintain it. This is particularly important for business executives and managers. In order to display and practice good interpersonal skills as a business person one must:

1. **Use the You-Attitude**: Putting readers or listeners first and being considerate to them and their needs.
2. **Demonstrating a positive attitude**: by creating a good working relations with colleagues, superiors, subordinates, and clients. Also showing interest in the job through cooperation and emotional constraints.
3. **Be a good listener**: Listening shows an interest in people and their views or opinion and is a quality of a good communicator.

4. **Maintain confidentiality**: Keeping confidential information confidential and avoiding spreading rumors even if it is the truth.

5. **Be Considerate**: Simply treat other people the way you want to be treated, with courtesy, honesty and patience.

The business communication principles

In order to help achieve effective communication the basic writing principles (also known as the C's of Business Communication) are applied to correspondences. The C's can apply to communication situations when speaking or writing, both in the case of external and internal communications. They make the communication logical and easy to understand.

The C's include:

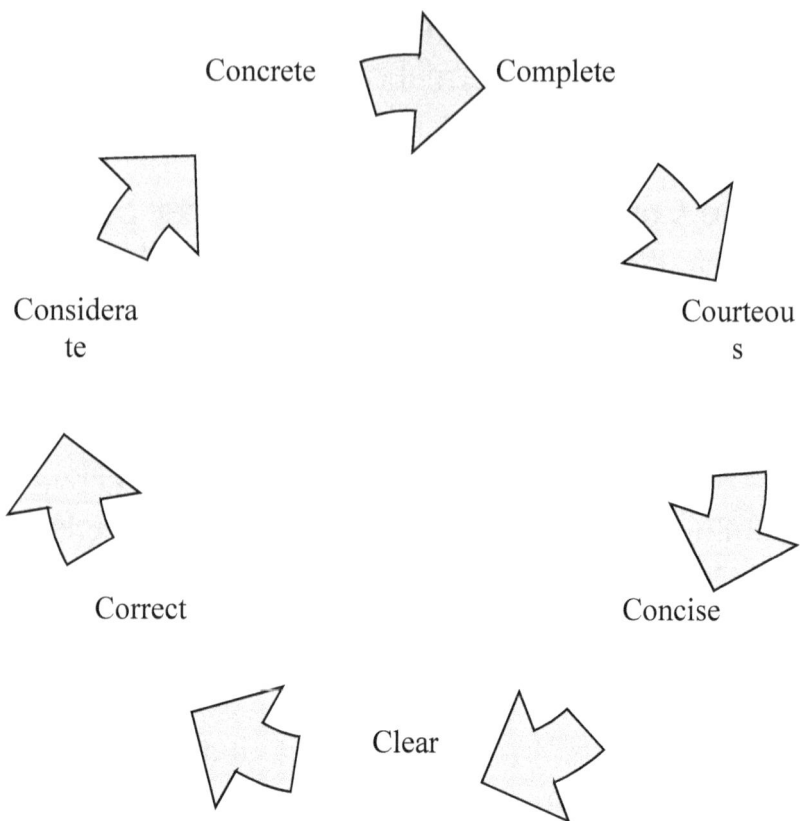

Concrete Complete

Considerate Courteous

Correct Concise

Clear

1. **Complete** – A complete communication must contain all the important information needed by the receiver for taking action; the details should be enough so that the receiver will not need to ask for more information. A message will be incomplete if essential information is not included. A good way to test the completeness of a message is to ask whether the 5W's and 1H has been attended to: who, what, where, when, why

and how. Complete messages tend to yield desired results.

2. **Courteous** – A courteous communication is polite, tactful, friendly, reader centered (you-attitude) and avoids irritating expression. The careful use of words must be observed to avoid words that may create unfavorable reaction. In short, putting oneself in the readers place. The organization is judged by the friendliness and consideration of its communication.

3. **Concise** – A concise communication using relevant facts to communicate the message in a clear and courteous manner. It is saying what you have to say in the fewest words possible, using only essential words and facts. Unnecessary words cluster the message and hamper the communication.

4. **Clear** – A clear communication is one that is easily understood and avoids any possible misunderstanding. It only contains short words and sentences. The communicators meaning should be clear and direct, with logical, consistent and unified flow, using simple words, short sentences, avoiding jargons and ambiguity.

5. **Correct** – A correct communication is accurate in every aspect (facts, timing, and style). Minor errors in dates, amount of

money or time may create a loss of time, money, goodwill or all three, verification of facts and attention to accuracy is a must. Typographic errors and sources of information should be verified, and grammar, spelling and punctuation should be correct.

6. **Consideration** – This is the preparation of a message with the recipient in mind and trying to be considerate to his or her educational level, culture, emotions, time, religion, sex, etc. focusing on the 'You-attitude', sincerity and emphasizing pleasant facts

7. **Concrete** – A concrete communication is a message that is specific, definite and vivid rather than being vague and general. It is using specific facts, figures, names and references to validate the communication. When all the above principles are observed, it is likely that the message is concrete.

Ethics of Business Communication

In business some things are legal but not ethical and these elements have an effect on business communication. Consumers can only make ethical choices about which organizations to do business with when they have access to correct and factual information about the practices of various businesses. Any business that aspires to be socially and ethically responsible must make it a priority to adopt ethical communication both internally and externally.

The benefits of being a socially responsible business is an advantage not only the owners of the business but also to the community and the natural environment in which the business operates. It is a belief that socially conscience businesses have a market advantage, because many consumers would prefer to do business with companies they consider ethical. The reality however is that consumers are often cynical about businesses due to the fact that they do not have access to credible information about the business practices of different organizations. Committing to both internal and external ethical communication allows customers know about what sets the organization apart from its contemporaries and sets an example on how businesses should operate. To be considered ethical a business should try to adopt the following:

1. **Treating others with honesty and fairness** - Ethics in business communication

is displayed honesty and fairness in the treatment of people, in short words treating others the way you would like to be treated. For example, not lying to clients to make quick money. Communication must be factually accurate, non-deceptive and complete. This applies to the areas of human resources, marketing and advertising, public relations, accounting among others.

2. **Stating facts instead of opinions** - Ethics requires that information communicated should be true, this is possible by using objective language and verifiable facts and information. This is especially important when the communication will be used as a basis to make decision.

3. **Making ethical communication** - Withholding information that can cause communication to be misinterpreted is a violation of ethical business communication. This means telling clients, employees or the public the negative effect of the product or services as well as the positive.

4. **Maintaining confidentiality** - Confidential informational are private or secrets and

should only be released to people with a proven need and authority to know. Right-to-privacy law is active in most nations this implies that records and communications of private nature must not be revealed. Examples of these include Medical records, attorney client files, banking and financial record, etc.

5. **Code of ethics** - Some organizations develop their code of ethics and make it public for both internal and external public in order to inform the public of their stance. The Code of ethics states how the organization conducts its business, how it treats customer and even competitors. Most businesses want to be held accountable to the code of ethics as a way to show their values.

It is a proven fact in business that ethical communication builds trust between all stakeholders including the company's employees, the owners, consumers or clients and the local community, while unethical communication abuses or damages trust. Businesses that demonstrate respect for human values and appreciate the different cultures in their communications can build trust with a broad spectrum of stakeholders and improve their reputation for being social responsible.

Communications in organizations

"To effectively communicate, we must realize that we are all different in the way we perceive the world and use this understanding as a guide to our communication with others."
-Anthony Robbins

"Good communication does not mean that you have to speak in perfectly formed sentences and paragraphs. It isn't about slickness. Simple and clear go a long way."
-John Kotter

Introduction

To ensure successful communications within your organization, it is best to start with the very basics: your knowledge of verbal and non-verbal communications. In the workplace, these types of communications are continually exchanged, oftentimes without much planning or even the thought that such communications are taking place.

Setting aside a specific time for meetings and regular communications is a great idea. This allows time for everyone involved to prepare. Also, keep in mind that listening is oftentimes much more productive when working to communicate effectively, and can very well be more important than talking. Allow everyone involved the time they need to communicate effectively.

Types and forms of communications in organizations

Communication in organizations can be complex and dynamic in nature. Organizational communication is the exchange of information and transmission of meaning among several individuals and communication in organizations can be distinguished into many categories, such as formal and informal communication; external and internal communication.

Internal Communication
Internal Communication is the transmission of information between and among employees of the organization or business. Internal communication is used to accomplish company goals and objectives. Internal communication may be carried out between people in the same department, other departments, and at other company locations. The employee can communication can individually or in groups. Internal communication may include face-to-face conversations, phone calls, e-mails, and brainstorming in meetings to mention a few. The tone of internal communication is normally friendly and informal in most organizations. The goals of internal communications in the order of their importance are: (1) to create the sense that employees are a significant asset to the organization; (2) to increase morale and promote goodwill between employees and management; (3) to update employees about internal changes; (4) to explain compensation and benefit plans; (5) to increase employee knowledge of the organization and its products, structure, ethics, culture, and external environment; (6) to transform employee

behavior toward becoming more productive, quality oriented, and entrepreneurial; (7) to improve employee understanding of major health/social issues or trend affecting them; and (8) to encourage employee partake in community activities.

External communication

External communication Is the transfer of information from and to the people out side the company. The goal of most external communication is to persuade the recipient to respond favorable to the organization. This communication can include sales letters to get potential customer, job listings (adverts) to attract qualified people most public relations communication. External communication has a more polite and formal tone than internal communication.

Formal communication

Formal communication are officially recognized and endorsed messages and information that is transmitted within the organization or externally, they include orders from superior to subordinates, statement to the general public, various written and unwritten reports, letters and other communication that is required in the daily running of the organization. They include both internal and external communication.

Informal communication
Informal communication consists of informal exchanges between employees or customers without a planned agenda. It is the form of communications that is not officially sanctioned and recognized by the organization, it is sometimes referred to as grapevine at times. It normally occurs when there are gaps in or barriers to formal communication and employees do not receive information they desire. Informal communication takes place by the water coolers, in the hall ways, company cafeterias, in employee's offices, in the parking lots, at restaurants, trade shows, etc. Topics like job opportunities, promotions, downsizing, competitors' products, unethical behaviors of managers, etc are normally discussed.

Informal communication has both its advantages and disadvantages. The negative effect is that gossips and rumors can be harmful to employee morale and motivation and ultimately the company performance. Exaggerate state of affairs such as downsizing can lead to high employee turnover and loss of key employees. On the other hand informal communication has been known to facilitate creative ideas and organizations. New product ideas have been developed over a bottle of cold beverages and fun conversation.

Formal Communication Networks
Other forms of communications that take place in organizations are influenced by the organizational structure in terms of their formal communication networks. The formal communication networks are more evident in bigger organizations and are structures developed by management to determine who should talk to whom to get a job done.

Organizational charts such as the one illustrated below help to explain formal communication networks:

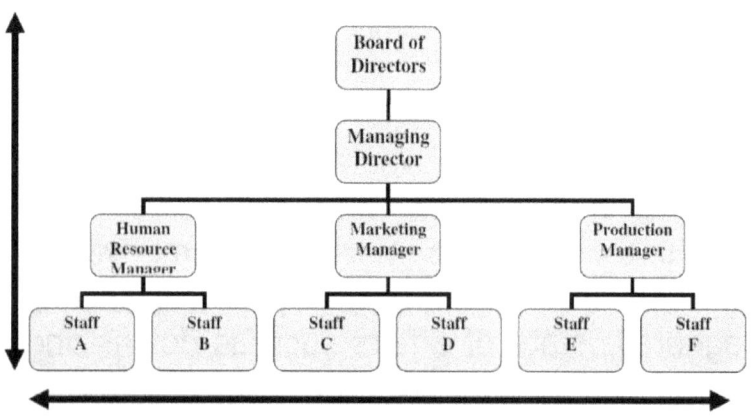

Vertical communication

Vertical communication is the upward and downward flow of communication in the organization, it is made up of the downward and upward communication and usually takes place along formal report line, between superiors and subordinates and may involve several levels of the organization.

Downward communication

Downward communication is a part of vertical communication; it is the process whereby information or messages is sent from a high position in the organization to an individual or group lower in the hierarchy (or organization chart). Downward communication constantly occurs between managers and subordinate, when manager provide direction, feedback, orders, assignment, policies and other critical information to help subordinates perform at expected levels. Examples include employee performance evaluation, job description, orientation or new employees, praise and recognition, company business strategy, goals and procedures.

Upward communication

Upward communication, this is the second part of vertical communication. It is when a message or information is sent from a position lower in the hierarchy to a receiver higher in the hierarchy. It helps managers know how individuals, teams and units of the company are performing, and enable him/her adjust according to responses. Upward communication facilitates feedback to managers about employees' feeling on the organization policies. Barriers that hinder upward communication includes the tendency of punishing the bearers of bad news, and the perception that taking problems over the head of immediate boss to his or her superior is considered disloyalty.

In order to overcome this situations companies can adopt an open-door policy which encourages any employee to bring the problems directly to the manager and the problem is dealt with within a specified period by the manager. Others use employee suggestion system to improve the product and process of quality. Effective use of upward communication enables employee air their suggestions, grievances, information about ethics, accounting information, information about defect rate of products, etc.

Horizontal communication

Horizontal communication is also called lateral communication, it occurs between individuals at a similar level in the organization. It is most likely to take place between team members, between different teams and between employees in different unit, such as between a safety specialist and a quality control specialist discussed possible changes in the production process.

Horizontal communication is becoming more and more important in organizations because it facilitates collaborations between employees with different skills and competencies. Horizontal communication facilitates the sharing of information between knowledge workers. Due to recent trends of downsizing and re-engineering organizations to be flatter and the advent of interactive electronic communication technologies, horizontal communication makes it possible to develop learning communities, and vital teams of employees working from different geographical locations. Examples of horizontal communication include peer assessment, cross-functional product development teams, self management work teams, suggestion committee meetings, and diversity task forces.

Communication Network patterns in Organizations

Communication networks influence groups in several important ways. Communication networks may affect the group's completion of the assigned task on time, the position of the de facto leader in the group, or they may affect the group members' satisfaction from occupying certain positions in the network. Although these findings are based on laboratory experiments, they have important implications for the dynamics of communication in formal organizations. There are several patterns of communication:

1. The Chain network can readily be seen to represent the hierarchical pattern that characterizes strictly formal information flow, "from the top down," in military and some types of business organizations (e.g. Assembly-line workers)

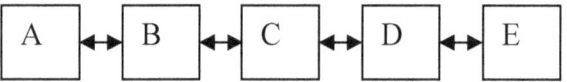

2. The Y network enables a leader (A) to share information at the same time through two channels (D and E). Who in turn pass on the information. This approach carries

information much faster than the chain network.

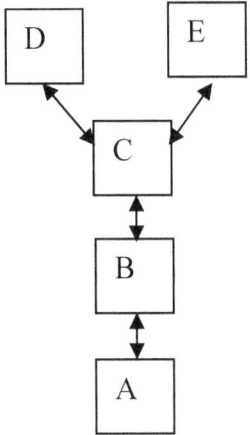

3. The Wheel (Star) network can be compared with a typical autocratic organization, meaning one-man rule and limited employee participation (e.g. Group leader to members).

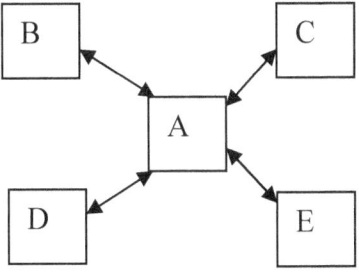

4. The Circle network is similar to the basic formal structure of many organizations. The

interaction is lateral and is typically found in autonomous groups (e.g. Taskforce members).

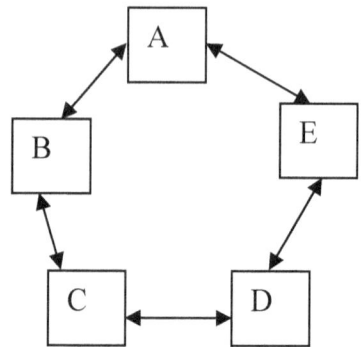

5. The All-Channel network ensures the free-flow of communication in a group that encourages all of its members to become involved in group decision processes. The All-Channel network may also be compared to some of the informal communication networks (example: Top-management team members e.g. Board of Directors).

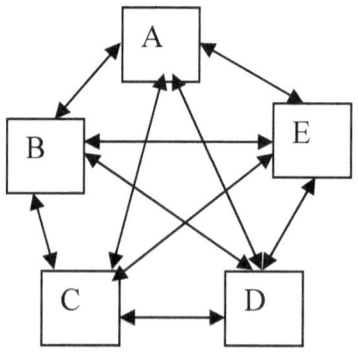

Nature of communication in an organization

Organization can improve the quality of communications by providing a diverse mix of high information richness channels that create opportunity for information flow vertically and horizontally. It is vital that management and staff are trained to use the types of communication channels appropriately. The upgrading of employee communication skills is also important due to the rapid changes in communication technologies and the global business culture. Below are types of communications that take place in an organization.

Face-to-face communication

Face-to-face communication provides opportunities for sending rich information content; it offers a high level of interactivity between the sender and receiver. Not only is verbal communication used but also the interpretation of each other's non verbal signals such as facial expressions and body language. Most job interviews are done face-to –face in order to asses the most suitable candidate accurately. One of the most important types of face-to-face communication is the meeting. Meetings are held to inform and train participants, solve problems, monitor and coordinate activities, delegate tasks and create social bond between organization members. The applications of multimedia technologies that transmit video, voice and text over satellite network have made face-to-face meetings with globally dispersed people possible. The importance of meetings highlights the use of the face-to-face channel.

Electronic communication
Electronic communication is communication that is transmitted over phone lines and satellite networks. Electronic communication through the advancement of technology makes interactive communication possible between senders and receivers who are separated by physical distance and busy schedules. Electronic communication channels vary in richness of the information that is transmitted and can include text, voice, graphic or video transmission. Electronic communications has been facilitated by the advancement of technology and adds to the impact of technology on communication in business. Electronic communication includes: voice mail,

cellular phones, pagers, facsimile machines (fax), scanners, computerized information system, personal computers, electronic mail, printers, modems, the internet and the world wide web, to mention a few. There are three most important forms of electronic communication used in business and they are:

1. **Voice mail** – Lets a sender transmit a detail audio message that is electronically recorded and can be played back when convenient or forwarded if needed. Voice mails also allow a sender to set up a menu of responses to commonly asked questions which saves on time and money. For example MTN Uganda uses voice mail to give information on loading airtime and checking balances. Sometimes voice mail become annoying when callers feel they are being screened and avoided by the business due to being placed on voicemail for too long.

2. **E-mail** – which is electronic mail allow employees to communicate via written messages through personal computer terminals linked to a network. E-mail is a very fast way to distribute information that is important about the business to a large number of employees at once. E-mail is often used to exchange information,

socializing and to post general notices that might be vital to individuals. E-mail has been used as a channel for upward communication in some organization, for example, Bill Gates, Chairman of Microsoft Corporation (and former CEO) made his address known to all Microsoft employees and personally replies their e-mails daily (for several reserved hours of course). The negative aspect of e-mail is that it can be a source of information overload, and at times excessive e-mail are sent to people who have no use for them. E-mails are not considered private due to the fact that several organizations have access to employee e-mails and monitor their activities.

3. **The Internet** – Is a computer network with multimedia communication capabilities, this means it can combine voice, graphics, and video to be sent to a receiver. Several organizations have websites on the internet where customers can get information on products and services and can place orders or ask questions. The use of the internet has made it possible for companies to serve international customers; universities like Kampala International University advertise their programmes on their

website to attract foreign students and electronic commerce has created a whole new business arena of opportunities, such as Amazon.com, BN.com, ebay.com, oneshare.com, etc where one can actually transact business online (on the internet) in the comfort of his/her house or office. The negative aspect of the internet is that it tends to generate information over load, computer viruses, fraudsters, Hackers and employees indulging on websites such as facebook, twitter, YouTube, pornographic pages and personal internet based e-mail accounts which ultimately lead to waste of company time and money.

Written communication

Written communication includes memos, policy manuals, employee handbooks, company newsletters, bulletin boards, letters and others. The advantage of written communication has over face-to face is that they can be revised, stored, made available when needed and identical copies can be made for handouts. Written communication can be personalized for a small audience or written in a general style to accommodate a large audience. The negative aspects of written communication is that there are no provisions for feedback and the sender will not be able to know if the message was received, read and understood. Written communications are used for the following reasons:

1. ***Conveying complex information*** – it can be written with the aid of graphs, illustrations and other visual data that aids understanding.

2. ***Reaching your intended reader*** – It could be easier to reach your reader by written correspondence due to no information on phone number.

3. ***Providing proof of the communication*** – for legal or reference purposes.

4. ***Ensuring confidentiality of information*** – some information cannot be relayed on phone and sometimes by e-mail, so a correspondence with 'confidential' or 'personal' may be more effective.

5. ***Providing convenience for the reader*** – He/she can read it at his/her time and any location.

6. ***Expediting the response to the communication*** – It would be effective to reply written correspondence with reference to the previous one to ensure clarity and completeness.

7. *Planning your message* – It allows you time to revise and organize your thoughts before expressing them.
8. *Saving time and money* – Written communication may be less expensive and time consuming than personal visits and phone calls.
9. *Stressing the importance of communication* – people may attach more importance and effort to letter written than phone calls. It can also display thoughtfulness.
10. *Aiding in distributing the same information to several people* – it is faster to photocopy written correspondence and send it to many individual than making calls or visits each at a time.
11. *Translating international communication* – it allows reader to translate correspondence properly and accurately in the case of foreign language correspondences than phone calls or face-to-face.

Nonverbal communication
Nonverbal communication Skills are essential for sending and decoding message with emotional content; friendliness, apologies,

respect, acceptance, rejection are only communicated effectively by nonverbal communication complimented by verbal communication. When the verbal and nonverbal communication disagree, the receiver is likely to pay attention to the nonverbal alone. Studies indicated that only 20% of our communication is verbal. The remaining 80% is non-verbal. Nonverbal communication includes:

1. ***Body movement and gestures*** – Posture can indicate attentiveness or lack of interest. Gesture can also add or detract from verbal messages; hand gestures can help emphasis points, but fidgeting signals that the speaker is nervous and lack confidence. Also different cultures place different meanings on gestures, like thumbs up is OK in USA, good in Britain and provocation in Brazil.

2. ***Eye contact*** – Indicate attentiveness or lack of interest on the part of the sender or receiver in a face-to-face conversations on the other hand prolonged eye contact may be interpreted as aggressiveness or inappropriate intimacy. Some cultures find making eye contact with elders or superiors to be rude, while a lack of eye contact in other cultures can indicate dishonesty. It is

wise to make eye contact sparingly in business conversations. (e.g. culture: China and Japan little or no eye contact with superior)

3. *Touch* – Indicates like, acceptance and friendship and is a very powerful signal. A firm handshake indicates enthusiasm and confidence while a weak one states otherwise. The use of touch in business has to be very cautious, unwanted touching in the USA can lead to complaint of sexual harassment. Some cultures encourage touch, like the French and kissing on the cheek when greet friends and business associates.

4. *Facial expression* – Reveals the emotional state of an individual such as fear, hate and confusion. A smile and firm hand shake is a good way to establish positive connection with a new acquaintance.

5. *Physical Distance* – Individuals regulate the physical distance between themselves and others while communicating. There is a tendency to stand close to friends, intimate partners and family, but further back with business and casual social acquaintances. Being too close or too far away from an individual can cause discomfort and a high

possibility of miscommunication. Different cultures have different acceptable standards, for example people in Venezuela tend to stand closer to business associates unlike in the U.S.A and backing away is considered rude in Venezuela when communicating.

6. ***Tone of voice*** – Such as pitch, loudness, speed and clarity of speech can indicate emotions such as attentiveness, friendliness, anger, or fear. In business communicating confidence is vital to build credibility, therefore it is wise to practice speaking clearly, emphasizing key words, and the use various speed to keep audiences interest and attentive. Talking in monotone will convey lack of interest and boredom, reducing the audiences' interest in listening to the verbal communication.

7. ***Personal Appearance*** – Appearance such as dress code, grooming and looks can create credibility that can better endorse effective communication. In fact research has proven that personal appearance plays a major role at job interviews and negotiations.

Be mindful of your own nonverbal cues, as well as the nonverbal cues of those around you.

Keep your messages short and concise. This means preparing in advance whenever possible. And for the spontaneous meeting, it means thinking before you speak.

Verbal communication in business

"Remember not only to say the right thing in the right place, but far more difficult still, to leave unsaid the wrong thing at the tempting moment."
— **Benjamin Franklin**

"A good speech should be like a woman's skirt; long enough to cover the subject and short enough to create interest."
— **Winston Churchill**

Oral Communication

Oral communication mainly refers to spoken verbal communication, but it can also utilize visual aids and non-verbal elements to facilitate the transmission of meaning. Oral communication includes speeches, presentations, discussions and aspects of interpersonal communication. Simply stated, oral communication is the process of expressing information or ideas by word of mouth. The strength of oral communication can never be over stated:

1. Oral communication is more personal and carries a less formal feel to it.
2. Oral communication is very effective in establishing quick resolutions when there are time constraints.
3. Oral communication is very flexible and responsive.
4. Oral communication is a very potent way to boost employee morale, enthusiasm and energy level.

On the down side, oral communication tends to be less thorough and more subject to misinterpretation than written communication.

Forms of oral communication

There are various forms of oral communication characterized by using verbal and non-verbal messages to generate meanings within and across various contexts, cultures, channels and media. According to concentric model of fields of communication introduced by Baden Eunson the different types of communication can be perceived in a linked and methodical way in the following manner:

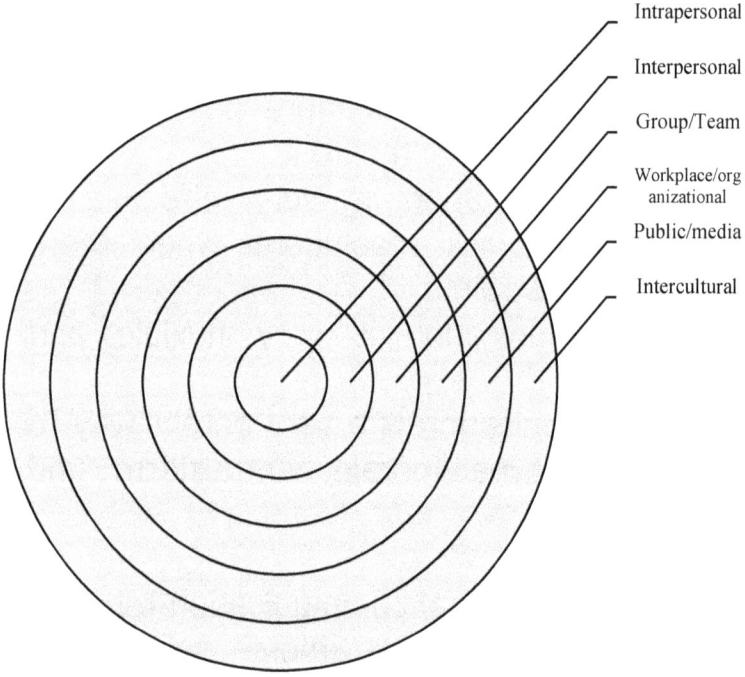

Intrapersonal

Interpersonal

Group/Team

Workplace/org
anizational

Public/media

Intercultural

The concentric model of fields of communication divides communication into six different levels and suggests that the more levels of communication that are utilized in any particular situation, the better the quality of communication would be.

Intrapersonal communication
Intrapersonal communication involves one person; it is a form of thinking that goes on inside a person which relies on language to express itself. It is self-talk or a conversation a person hold within them yourself under certain circumstances. A person can communicate to himself or herself through pain, thinking, feelings or emotions.

Interpersonal communication
Interpersonal communication is communication between several people. This form of communication may range from the formal and impersonal to intimate and very personal. Impersonal communication is when talking with a person who is only a business associate and only have a formal relationship with. While carrying on a conversation with a loved one, sharing a serious concern can be considered intimate or very personal. Intimate communication tends to have more emotional content attached to it than impersonal communication. Dyadic communication, which

is an aspect of interpersonal communication, involves two people. An example is when a couple is chatting.

Group communication
Group communication takes place in a group, typically consisting of five to 10 people. The larger the group, the more likely it is to break down into smaller groups or subgroups. This form of communication serves relationship needs such companionship, family bonding and affection or support. In organizations groups may convene to discuss issues related to work, such as problem-solving, product development or team-building.

Organizational communication
Organizational communication, also known as corporate communication, deals with communication within large organizations such as businesses. It is characterized by the interactions between employees and employers in organizations. Successful organizational communications enhances corporate image and has a positive effect on morale, commitment, and productivity in organizations. In some cases organization communication has been used interchangeably with group communication.

Public communication

Public communication is also known as public speaking, it involves communication between a speaker and an audience. This audience may range from just a few people to millions of people. In simple terms it is one person speaking to a group of people. Public communication is characterized by information sharing, entertainment or persuasions to make the audience act, buy or think in a certain way. An example is the marketing manager talking to everyone in the sales team, and the sales team silently listening without interrupting.

Mass communication

Mass communication is a more public form of communication between an individual and a large and varied audience, mediated by some form of technology. The channel used is through media like films, radio, videos and television. The audiences' feedback is limited or delayed. New technologies of mass communication like the Internet and blogs are very potent since information is disseminated instantly and feedbacks are faster. Business communicators can use multimedia channels such as visual aid or films, or other images to advertise or transmit a message globally.

International communication

International communication, also known as cross cultural, transnational and global communication, is the communication practice that is transmitted across international borders. This can take the form of organizations from various foreign nations interacting with each other. The need for international communication is influenced by the rapid increase in globalization and international business and trade. In business, cross cultural communication plays a critical role in successfully carrying out business across the globe. It can help to enhance institutional knowledge and competitive advantage.

Public Speaking

Studies have shown that some people are more scared of public speaking than of dying, studies have also shown that one of the most admired qualities in others is the ability to speak in front of a group with confidence and eloquence. The ability to speak confidently in front of a crowd or group is a major consideration when employers are looking for a new employee.

Public speaking is simply addressing a group with the intention of influencing their opinion, inform, ordering, teaching, etc. Any communication made in front of an audience is public speaking. It is important to understand that nonverbal communication plays a significant role in public speaking, such as dress code, nervousness, body movement, eye contact, etc. There are several types of public speaking:

Briefing: Briefings are concise and factual communication to the audience. Briefings are most commonly used in military organizations. There are four types of briefings: (i) information briefing, (ii) decision briefing, (iii) mission briefing and (iv) staff briefing (general briefing). Briefings are informative, directing, advocating, or persuading. Every good briefing follows the ABC principle: Accuracy, Brevity, Clarity. Accuracy and clarity characterizes all good public speaking, but brevity distinguishes briefings from any other form of public speaking.

Lecturing: Lecturing can be defined as a communication on a given subject delivered before an audience, a congregation or a class for the purpose of instruction. This is commonly used in educational institutions and religious institutions such as churches and mosques. The communication is directed towards instructing, teaching and informing. Lectures can also be divided into two sub categories:

1. **Formal Lectures** are by nature one sided with no verbal contribution from the audience e.g. during a sermon.
2. **Informal Lectures** are normally presented to small audiences and allowing verbal interaction between the instructor and the audience.

Speech: A speech is defined as a formal communication delivered to an audience. Speeches have one of the following purposes to achieve, to inform, to persuade, or to entertain. There are several types of speeches:

1. **Informative Speech** is a narration concerning a specific topic, but does not involve a sustained effort to teach. This kind of speech you would be delivering facts and statistics. An example of informative speech is an orientation talk for students (freshers); the whole talk informs the new students on how things work in their new environment.

2. **Persuasive Speech** is designed to move the audience to believe or act on the topic. These speeches are used by salespeople and politicians, with the aim of getting the audience to buy a specific product, vote or donate money to a cause.
3. **Entertaining Speech** is focused at giving enjoyment to the audience; the speaker often relies on the use of stories, humor and vivid language as primary means of entertaining the listeners and delivering the key points. Example of this type of talk includes presentations and standup comedy. They are deliberately used to induce sensory recall. This type of speech is the most effective when delivering any message, but is the most difficult to make because it requires skills and talent which a majority might not possess.
4. **Inspirational Speech** is aimed at motivating and challenging the audience to the best they can be. An example these speeches are made at high school graduations, inaugural addresses. A more practical example is the famous 'Yes we can' speech by Barrack Obama.

When developing a speech, choose a general speech purpose for your topic and make it very clear both at the opening as well as the conclusion of your speech. The body of the speech is similarly vital and many of the other types of speeches can be included to prevent boredom and engaging the audience. For example an inspirational speech is more powerful when combined with some facts and some light humor, similarly an informative speech would be more palliative to listen to with entertaining anecdotes included.

Presentation Skills

In simple terms a presentation is an undertaking in which a person (the presenter) shows, describes, or explains something to a group of people. Most professionals, including those in business, occasionally make presentations to students, employees, clients, etc. It is a fact that people in business will have to make presentations, even those at lower levels in the organization. It is therefore important that presentation skills are developed and the best way to do this is through practice. The following is a guide to enhance presentations skills.

Preparing for a presentation: The importance of preparation cannot be emphasized enough when it comes to making a presentation. Preparation includes analyzing the audience in order to know how to develop and deliver the speech or information to the audience in a way that will suit the specific audience (this includes clarity, content, humor, language, etc). Preparation will make the difference between successfully getting through to your audience in the aspect of their time and attention and ultimately influencing their decision or not.

Creating visual aids: In order to facilitate effective communication, reduce boredom and confusion the use of visual aid is always a benefit to presentations. They do not replace the presentation, but they act as a tool for facilitating understanding. Visual aids can include samples of products, power points projection, slips, hand outs, videos, demonstrations, etc. It is a proven fact that presentations that use visual aid are about 43% more persuasive than those that don't. In addition visual aids help the audience to remember what the presentation was about.

Displaying a professional Image: It is important to know that when you are going to deliver your message on the podium, people are forming their opinion about you and what you are going to talk about. A big part of the opinion is based on how you look, dress, talk and walk. This mean being dressed professionally, looking well groomed, being realistic, using good mannerisms, display confidence and make proper introductions, among other things.

Delivering presentation: The successful delivery of a good presentation is built on preparation and how well it is delivered. The following are helpful guides:

1. Don't read the presentation; summarize it in a manner that engages the audience. Reading will make you lose your audience and leave them bored and disinterested.
2. Radiate a positive energy, because it is contiguous and shows your passion or interest in what you are talking about.
3. Maintain eye contact with audience, because it shows honesty and sincerity. It makes the audience know you are talking to them and are worth listening to.
4. Speak slowly and occasionally pause to allow audiences absorb the information. Though speaking slightly faster, but understandable can audiences more attentive; it is important to allow moments

of pauses for them to digest the information. Speaking too slowly will make your audience fall asleep.

5. Use accurate grammar to avoid distraction and awkward moments during the presentation. The excessive use of inaccurate grammar can lead to the audience switching off and not taking your presentation seriously.

6. Be audible, because it shows that you are confident and know what you are talking about.

7. Never turn your back on the audience for a long period. This will make you lose your audience and disengage their interest.

8. Engage the audience by interacting with them through humor, brief simple questions and walking among the audience (if the location makes it possible).

9. Repeat important points to help the audience remember them.

10. Avoid clichés and sounds such as 'ums', 'uhhs', because they make the audience lose interest and show that you are not prepared.

11. Anticipate noise in the audience and try to take charge by pausing to let them know they are disturbing.

12. Stay within your time limit and live time for question from the audience.

Managing Stage Fright: Symptoms of stage fright can include cold hands, sweaty palms, shaky knees or hands, quivering voice and a pounding heart to mention a few. Stage fright is a natural emotion; all speakers experience stage frights, but experienced speaker convert this energy into a positive one. Most people list stage fright above the fear of dying and of snakes. Experienced speakers live with stage fright by learning how to manage it. Stage flight is normally caused due to our mostly unfounded fears; such as fear of failure, embarrassment, losing control, being judged, not being perfect, disappointing our superiors, showing our weaknesses, exposing our ignorance, looking like idiots, being laughed at or going "blank."

The anxiety can be managed by the following suggestions:
1. Preparing adequately.
2. Master the information to be delivered.
3. Prepare a very strong opening due to the fact that fright starts then.
4. Try to talk with members of the audience before the presentation to ease the tension.

5. Relax and loosen up by doing simple exercise.
6. Before getting to the podium take three deep breaths to help relax your nerves.
7. When speaking focus only on your topic and your audience, nothing else.
8. Develop a positive attitude towards public speaking by practicing and making the most of less formal speaking opportunities.

Meetings

Face to face communication among people in an organization is unavoidable and essential to the business meetings and is important in business communications because meeting tend to achieve more results than phone calls, letters, or electronic mail. Meetings are one of the most important ways of exchanging ideas and information in business. Meetings can involve superiors, and employees, several levels of the organization, employees and customers, etc. Meetings can be called depending on the urgency, the topic, the number of participant, and their ability to make it on time. While meetings are magnificent tools for generating ideas, expanding on thoughts and managing group activity, this face-to-face contact with team members and colleagues is more likely to fail without adequate preparation and leadership.

Meetings allow employers and employees to communicate and exchange information, solve problems or resolve disputes, enforce teamwork, enhance performance, and progress on projects. Meetings can be formal or informal, and the number of participants can range from two to several hundred, depending on the size of the company and the nature of the meeting. Meetings are held for the following reasons, in most case:

1. to share information with others in the organization
2. to discuss new ideas and proposals and vote on it
3. to involve employee in daily business and interest them
4. to do collective problem solving and brainstorming
5. to give feedbacks on activities
6. to help coordinate activities
7. to sort out any conflicts.
8. to negotiate a contract or agreement, or matters to do with it.
9. to receive a report for assessment and review.

There are several types of meetings in today's business world; they can be characterized by their structure or purpose among others. Examples include problem-solving meeting, decision making meeting, planning meeting and feedback meeting. Generally meetings can be divided into several categories such as stated below.

Formal Meetings: Formal meetings are preplanned, structured and usually conducted by an elected official. Formal meetings follow strict procedures which mean a set of rules for conducting the meeting has to be observed. Example of these types of meetings includes annual or quarterly corporate meetings of directors, executives or shareholders. Another example are conventions for professional bodies.

Informal Meetings: Informal meeting include staff meetings, management meetings, and project team meetings, all these meetings are held when needed and they tend to follow a discussion format, with an individual serving as a facilitator or coordinator and another person serving as a note taker.

Electronic Meetings: Electronic meeting are becoming more and more a part of business. It is the combined use of audio, video and other computer equipments, with several people in various locations communicating through these devices. Such meetings can be conducted cheaply and conveniently be using applications such as Skype and Face Time among other. The advancement in communication technology implies that various forms of meetings can even take place on the move with the help of tablets and smart phones.

The Importance of Preparation for meetings

To ensure everyone involved has the opportunity to provide their input, start your meeting off on the right foot by designating a meeting time that allows all participants the time needed to adequately prepare. Once a meeting time and place has been designated, make yourself available for questions that may arise as participants prepare for the meeting. If you are the meeting leader, make a meeting agenda, complete with detailed notes.

In these notes, outline the goal and proposed structure of the meeting, and share this with the participants. This will allow all involved to prepare and to come to the meeting ready to work together to meet the goals at hand. The success of the meeting is hinged on the skills displayed by leader. To ensure the meeting is successful, the leader should:

- Generate an agenda and make it available to all those involved in the meeting.
- Start the discussion and encourage active participation by asking the views and inputs of the respective members.
- Work to keep the meeting at a comfortable pace by not moving too fast or too slow.
- Summarize the discussion and the recommendations at the end of each logical section of the meeting.
- Circulate minutes to all participants after the meeting.

While these tips will help ensure meetings are productive and well-received, there are other important areas that need to be considered to make sure meetings and negotiation skills are fine tuned and ready to take to the meeting room.

Managing a Meeting
Choosing the right participants is vital to the success of any meeting. This means choosing

people who have the information and knowledge needed in the meeting. Make sure all participants can contribute and choose good decision-makers and problem-solvers. It is important to try and keep the number of participants to a maximum of 12 if not fewer.

The leader must work thoroughly to ensure that everyone's thoughts and ideas are heard by guiding the meeting so that there is a free flow of debate with no individual dominating. In addition no extensive discussions should take between sub groups within the meeting. When an agenda item is resolved or action is agreed upon, make it clear who in the meeting will be responsible for this. In an attempt to avoid confusion and misunderstandings, summarizing the action to be taken and including it in the meeting's minutes will be helpful.

Agenda: An agenda is the plan for a meeting. It acts as a guidance tool that keeps the participants of the meeting on the issues at hand in order to attain the desired objective. It helps participant to understand what is expected of them. An agenda identifies the objectives of the meeting, prepares participants for the meeting and defines the times allotted to each of the topics, and the order of discussion. A meeting without an agenda is most likely bound to be unproductive.

Minutes: A record of the proceedings in a meeting is called minutes. A note taker (secretary) is important in the meeting it is his or her job to take down the minutes. Minutes record the decisions of the meeting and the actions agreed. They provide a record of the meeting and, importantly, they provide a review document for use at the next meeting so that progress can be measured. Minutes are useful in identifying individual performance and non-performance on the basis of agreed actions from previous meeting.

The style of the minutes issued depends on the situation. In circumstances were record of the meeting is very vital, detailed minutes will be needed. Where this is not the case, then minutes can be simple lists of decisions made and of actions to be taken with the responsible person identified. Generally, minutes should be as short as permissible without leaving out vital information. This makes them quick and easy to prepare and utilize. It is ideal to issue the minutes of the meeting within 24 hours to facilitate quick reaction and engagement of delegated tasks.

Participating in Teams, Groups and Meeting

In business, group thinking and team work is integral to planning, decision making and problem solving. Many business groups, teams and committees are organized in order to harness the talents, ideas and skills of employees.

As a group or team member it is vital to understand group and team dynamics this will help to understand the attitudes and practices that hinder group effectiveness and performance.

The attitudes and practices of the following types of people hinder the success of meetings, group and team work:

- **Self Interest Pleader** – Everything he or she says and does is intended to help him or her get his or her way, despite the good ideas of others. These individuals tend to be persuasive and sometimes assertive. They will always want to justify why their way is the best and possibility the only way. The self interest pleader can show up to the meeting claiming to have all the solutions.

- **The Traditionalist** – This individual is always opposing new ideas and believes in tradition and the old way of doing this. Does not like innovation or thinking out of the box. In most cases these individual do not like change and will use the excuse of 'not fixing what is not broken'. The traditionalist can show up to the meeting wonder why there is need for a meeting, since all is going fine.

- **The Bully** – This individual is never aware of other people's feeling and in some cases does not care about their feelings. He or she tries to build his or her ego by undermining other people. They tend to feel superior and try to manipulate others in the group. Bullies can use their position or talent to intimidate others. The bully might come to the meeting to show off and shoot down people's ideas.

- **The Pity Seeker** – These individuals seek other people's sympathy and never want to accept responsibility or fail to carry through on their responsibility. Such persons would like the group to compliment their weaknesses. Pity seekers can use their lack of experience, young age, gender or being a minority as an excuse. The pity seeker might show up with no updates or feedbacks on tasks assigned from previous meeting.

- **The 'Whatever' person** - These individuals display of lack of interest or involvement and in some cases through cheeky tactics he or she may try to disrupt the group. In some cases might just give the group a frozen smile and agree with everything in order to mentally escape to 'boring' proceedings. These individuals lack motivation or feel they are being undermined. The 'whatever' person might show up late and want to leave early.

As a group or team member, try not to be one of these characters and try to observe them in the group in order to manage them especially if you are the leader.

Teleconferencing

A teleconference is a telephone meeting among two or more people involving technology more complex than a simple two-way phone connection. At its simplest, a teleconference can be an audio conference with one or both ends of the conference sharing a speaker phone. Teleconferencing allows people in different locations and time zones to meet electronically. Teleconferencing is sometimes referred to as electronic meeting, audio conferencing or video conferencing. In fact there are several types of teleconferencing:

1. **Audio Teleconference:** Voice-only; sometimes called conference calling. It interactively connects people in remote locations by telephone lines.

2. **Audiographics Teleconference**: Uses narrowband telecommunications channels to transmit visual information such as graphics, alphanumeric, documents, and video pictures as an adjunct to voice communication.

3. **Computer Teleconference**: Uses telephone lines to connect two or more computers and modems. Anything that can be done on a computer can be sent over the network using local area network (LAN) or wide area network (WAN).

4. **Video Teleconference**: Also known as videoconferencing. It combines audio and video to provide voice communications and video images.

The cost is determined by the time spent on using the equipment and of course the initial cost of purchasing the equipment. Many large companies can afford teleconferencing facilities, but small companies normally rent the teleconferencing services. Their benefits can never be understated:

1. **Reduces Travel**: One of the most significant advantages of teleconferencing is the reduced travel. Businesses with several offices can hold meeting and share critical information with employees through teleconferencing.
2. **Saves Time:** Teleconferencing save time. Time saved from reduced travel can be utilized more productively to finish tasks and carry out assigned roles respective locations.
3. **Reduce Costs:** Teleconferencing has realized a return to popularity as an effective tool for communication due to economic downturns. Companies report significant savings in travel and associated costs.
4. **Improved Productivity:** Teleconferencing allows better employee engagement through communication with coworkers at headquarters, conduct long-distance meetings and strategic discussions, and share grievances. This has led to a better understanding of roles and effective use of time which leads to enhanced productivity.

5. **Quick and short notice Scheduling:** Teleconferencing systems and toll-free, dial-in access facilities make it possible for companies to schedule short-notice or ad-hoc employee teleconferencing meetings or discussions. This is especially true with the use of internet based tools such as Skype among others.

Teleconferencing (audio conferencing): Audio teleconferencing initially called conference call is the cheapest, simplest and most commonly used form teleconferencing. All that is needed is a telephone or a speaker phone and the conference feature which is used to connect all the parties. Audio Conferencing normally used to exchange information, give directives, resolve minor conflicts, conduct collaborative problem solving, and present simple proposals. It remains less effective in comparison to face-to-face meetings. However basic technology such as mobile phones with speaker function can be used for teleconferencing, although it might not be the ideal.

Videoconferencing: Though it has been in existence since the 1970s, videoconferencing became more prominent in business in the

1990s, due to the need to cut on travel costs. It uses all media (audio, graphic and video). In most organizations a specific rooms is specially equipped cameras, monitors, multiple microphones, and special transmission lines for transmitting audio and video information. Less financially capable organizations have to rent rooms and equipments off location to utilise videoconferencing. A key advantage of videoconferencing is that it enables face-to-face communication (encouraging the use of nonverbal communication as well). Videoconferencing is normally used for product presentations, new-product announcements, personnel training and brainstorming sessions. Videoconferencing works better with a small group due to the fact that it is easy for others to get distracted if the group is large.

Dealing with the public
Most organizations have specific employees to deal and receive the public, such as the customer care, receptionist and the public relations officer. All employees at one point or the other have to deal with individuals from the public, such as clients and associates. Good customer and people skills are important not only for the sales people but for everyone in the organization. It is therefore vital that basic

procedures for meeting the public are understood. The following are the basics as recommended by Small Business BC:

1. **Listen:** Sometimes, customers just need to know that you're listening. This means giving prompt attention and being pleasant.

2. **Apologize:** When something goes wrong, apologize. Don't try to justify or give excuses when the fault is truly yours.

3. **Take them seriously.** Make customers feel important and appreciated. This means offering them a seat while they wait, asking how you can help when passing in the lobby and seeing that they are attended to as soon as possible.

4. **Stay calm.** Difficult as it is sometimes, it is important to stay calm. Never show clients that you are nervous, suspicious or angry. Be professional.

5. **Identify and anticipate needs.** Most customer needs are emotional rather than logical. Assure customers and even pat their ego if needed.

6. **Suggest solutions.** Have a menu of calming remedies which you and your colleagues can use. Always after an alternative if the first option fails.

7. **Appreciate the power of "Yes".** Always look for ways to help your customers. Show

them they are not a burden, but a pleasure to deal with.

8. **Acknowledge your limits.** Yes is a powerful word but if you're unable to fulfill a request: know your limits. Be honest by letting them know what you are capable of as an employee or company and what you are not.

9. **Be available.** Customer service is no longer just about face-to-face contact and telephone. Go the extra mile for your clients by acknowledging events such as Christmas, anniversary, etc by sending them cards or greetings.

10. **Get regular feedback.** Feedback is a great way to grow both your people and business skills. This means deliberately trying to find out how well you are doing from your clients and what they would like to see improved.

Employment Interviews

The job interview is a crucial part of your job search because it's an opportunity for the employer to figure out if you're right for the job. The job interview may be the most critical factor in determining whether a candidate is employed or not. No matter how impressive your background, your CV, and application letter, the inability to "sell" yourself might still lead to unemployment. In an interview you have the opportunity to sell yourself every time you speak through your response to questions, your descriptions of experiences and activities, your explanation of procedures and methods- all contribute to the interview impression.

Preparing a curriculum vitae

A curriculum vitae (CV), is an alternative to a resume. A resume is a one or two page summary of a person's skills, experience and education, while a CV is more detailed and longer. CVs were originally used by those in academia and research, but it is now common in job application and in some cases more popular than resumes. This is no specific style or format for a CV, it calls a little originality.

- **Length:** Most CVs are at least two pages long, unlike résumés that are about a page.
- **Font and Size:** Times New Roman, Arial, Calibri, or a similar font is best, with a font size of 10 or 12. Fancy fonts make the CV look unprofessional. The name and headings can be larger fonts and bolded.
- **Format:** The key thing is uniformity and consistency; there is no universal format for a CV.

- **Accuracy:** Accuracy is vital and so extra efforts must be placed to make sure spelling, grammar, tenses, names of companies and people, etc are correct.

Though there is no standard format for a CV, there are however, key things that have to be included in a CV. They include:

1. **Contact information** - include your name and contact information, such as address, phone number, email address, etc. and personal information, such as gender, date of birth, and marital status.
2. **Education** - Include the school attended, dates of study, and degree received
3. **Honors and Awards** - departmental awards, scholarships, fellowships, and membership in any honors associations
4. **Thesis/Dissertation** (for those in academia) - include a brief sentence or two on your paper, and/or the name of your advisor.
5. **Research Experience** (for those in academia) – include research positions held
6. **Work Experience** - List the employer, position, and dates of employment.

7. **Teaching Experience** (for those in academia) - Include the school, course name, and semester.
8. **Skills -** include language skills, computer skills, administrative skills, etc
9. **Publications and Presentations** (for those in academia) - List any publications you have written, co-written, or contributed to, along with papers presented.
10. **Professional Memberships** - List any professional associations you a member of.
11. **Extracurricular Activities** - Include any volunteer or service work
12. **References** - include the name, title, and contact information for those people who have agreed to be a reference for you. Three references are ideal.

Preparation for the interview

Though most people are not conscious of it at the time, the preparation for the job interview began a long time ago. When they chose the type of work they wanted to do, they acquired the education and training needed for the chosen career and finally targeting potential employers. That led to the compilation of a CV, list of reference, an application letter and ultimately the interview. To prepare for a job interview the following should be considered:

- *Remember the goal of the interview* – to market yourself and to find out if the job fits your qualification, personality and career plans.
- *Research the prospective employer* – Find out all you can about the company, its products and services, history and key individuals in management. Identify what its philosophy and core values are. This will help you decide whether it is the place for you and give you an advantage before the interview.
- *Prepare questions to ask the interviewers* – Ask question about the company's services and products, its performance, opportunities for advancement, HR policies, etc. All the questions asked should reflect your research on the company. This will create a good impression. Avoid questions that focus too much on salaries, pay raise, leaves, lunch hours and holidays. It might give the impression that you are only interested in the job for the money.
- *Know your strength and weaknesses* – Amplify your strength and try to manage your weaknesses by stated what you are

doing about them. This means you should emphasis your qualifications, experiences, skills and characteristics that will make you the right candidate for the job. Make sure you know your qualification and all the details about yourself off head. Always refereeing to your documents to get information about yourself might indicate you are lying to the interviewers. Never lie!

- *Anticipate Questions* – Be prepared to answer questions on you qualifications, education, past work experiences, hobbies, why you chose the profession, the organization, etc.

- *Be knowledgeable about the industry trends and current events* – Displaying knowledge of the industry and current events in your interview and their effects on the organization, the position and yourself once employed. This will make the interviewers impressed and interested in your abilities. They will feel that you will fit in the organization quickly.

- *Confirm your appointment* – Make sure you know the time it begins and when you are expected to arrive. Showing up late give a very bad impression.

- *Get direction to the interviewing site* – Make sure you know the location and how to get there on time. This means you have to factor in traffic and the means of transportation to get there.

- *Identify items to take to the interview* - Know what to take along for the interview e.g. original documentations, pen, paper, etc. Not coming prepared will give the impression that you are disorganized.
- *Get a good night's sleep before the day of the interview* – Get enough rest and relaxation before the day of the interview. This allows you to be at your best and look composed.

The Interview

At the interview it is important to remember to:

- Make a positive impression by arriving early, dressed professionally, demonstrating self confidence, and professionalism. Look and smell good, but avoid being excessive with your grooming.
- Greet interviewers with a firm hand shake and smile, and follow their cue to seat, to talk, to present documentation, etc.
- Let your personality shine by showing them your truly good qualities and values, without being unprofessional.
- Be attentive to interviewers and speak clearly for them to understand. Do not be

too wordy or talkative by going off the point.

- Remember the impact of nonverbal communication on the interview. Don't look like you are begging for the job.
- Be frank, honest and express confidence in yourself and your abilities. But do not be arrogant.
- Clearly point out what you can offer to the organization and what makes you unique.
- At the conclusion of the interview, thank the interviewers and let them know you will be waiting to hear from them.
- Be positive and optimistic

Business etiquettes
A big part of any business interaction is nonverbal communication. A positive nonverbal communication can yield favorable results at meetings, negotiations, interviews, etc. Business etiquettes are subtle but significant behaviors that can make or break an important meeting, influence a first impression or impress a potential client. Business etiquette is a code of behavior that portrays standards for social behavior according to contemporary norms within a society, social class, or group in the context of doing business. The following are some key factors to consider when trying to

comply with business etiquette. Good business etiquette is about making a good impression, treating people well, communicating affectively, and creating a favorable environment around you.

Make a positive impression
People normally forge their first impressions about others in a few seconds. It is therefore important that on first meetings it is crucial to make certain that you are appropriately prepared to present yourself as a professional. Business etiquette on creating a good impression includes:

- Standing upright, making eye contact, facing people when speaking to them, and sincerely smile at people.
- Complying with office dress code.
- Making sure your briefcase or bag is neat, organized and presentable.
- On meeting a person for the first time give a firm hand shake.
- Avoid falling asleep at work; it looks very bad.
- Always try to be kind and show courtesy to both client and workmates.
- Always show up to work on time.

Dealing with people

Treating people well and with respect will have an effect on how well you succeed in an organization. How you treat people tells a lot about what type of person, workmate or leader are. Business etiquette on dealing with people includes:

- Learn people's names quickly; by not knowing people's names it is perceived that you don't value that person. If you have a bad memory, write down the names.

- Resist making value judgments on people's significance in the workplace. Treat everybody with respect and don't only talk to the people that 'matter', talk to everyone.

- Evaluate how you treat your bosses, colleagues and subordinates and see if the different ways you interact with them will make others perceive you as being shallow.

- Limit what you share at work about your personal life and similarly don't try to forcefully know what is going on in other people's private life. Being workmates doesn't mean you are best friends.

- Give people their space at work and allow them to get their job done. Don't stand on the shoulder of subordinates or try to show people how to do their job.

Etiquettes of communicating

Communication is not just about speaking; it is more about what you don't say, what you do and how you say what you say. Business etiquette on communicating includes:

- Making sure you respond to phone calls and emails within 24 hours. Even if it is just to acknowledge that you got the message and will be reacting to it soon.
- Get consent of the person you are talking to before putting them on speakerphone.
- Personalize your voice mail to help callers know that they have reached your number.
- Office emails should be treated formally and characterized by sound grammar and spelling.
- Never use offensive words, aggressive or loud voice tone to address people at work, no matter what the position of the person is.

Etiquettes in meetings

The environment of a meeting demands some delicate projection in order to maintain your professional image. Whether the meetings are with superiors, workmates subordinates or with clients etiquettes can make a significant difference. Business etiquettes in meetings include:

- Arriving not more than five minutes early if the meeting is in someone else's office. This gives them time to prepare and get ready for the meeting. In simple terms, don't come too early, but never be late.
- If you are running late or planning to be late, inform the organizer of the meeting as early as possible. Being on time for a meeting means showing 5 minutes early, while for an interview it means arriving 10 minutes early.
- If the meeting is taking too long and you have to be somewhere else, always be ready to elucidate where you need to be because it will influence how you will be judged for leaving the meeting before it ends.
- Avoiding interrupting people and allow others to speak, contribute or give feedbacks.
- Avoid carrying out confrontations at meetings. It is the wrong place to do so. It will make you look bad and embarrass and annoy others.
- Allow people time and space outside of meetings to reflect on issues that need to be resolved.

Work space etiquette

A big chunk of our time is spent at work and can contribute to our sense of identity and belonging. This means that office space is vital for determining a good working environment and ultimately our overall mood and attitude. Work space etiquettes include:

- Keeping the space professional organized and neat with suitable individual touches. How your office space looks is a reflection of who you are.

- Respect other people's space. Wait to be invited into others office space, knock or make your presence gently known and always follow the lead of the owner of the office space you are in.

- Don't assume that because you are a superior you can seat behind a subordinates desk when you are in his or her office.

- Don't interrupt people who are on the phone. It is wiser to communicate with them in any form after they are done.

- Always avoid excessive personal calls. It is an abuse of office time and resources.

- Use mobile phones in the right place and time in the office. For example don't start making call in the middle of a meeting.

- Eat at the right place and time. The smell and noise associated with food can be distracting and it would be especially strange in a client walks into your office and it smell like a restaurant.

International business etiquette

It is hard of a business to be local in our contemporary business world. This is because of globalization. It means that one way or the other businesses people have to interact with others from other countries or cultures. This interaction might include foreign workmate, supplier, clients or even governments. This requires the need to understand numerous international standards of business etiquette. It also calls for business people to investigate the country they will be working in or visiting and learn the appropriate etiquette, culture and customs for that country. It is however important to note the following when conducting business internationally:

- Understanding the local language makes a good impression on the people you are doing business with. While pretending to know the language can create the opposite effect.
- Avoiding making international calls without understanding the time difference. Waking a business associate, setting unrealistic deadlines or raising a concern at awkward

hours can all reflect negatively on you. It can show lack of professionalism and outright disrespect in some cultures.

- It is important to note that working days and hours can vary from country to country and this should be put into consideration when making international business plans, such as meetings and calls.

- Show respect of local cultures, holidays and beliefs. Don't try to undermine or show that they are less important compares to the business dealings.

- Understand the etiquettes for meals, socializing and other events within cultures foreign to you to avoid a negative international business etiquette impression. These cultures are very significant to individuals in various countries and can prove costly when they are ignored or undermined. For example in an Arab country, you don't want to serve alcohol or pork to your guests.

Carefully scrutinize the business cultures in which you operate in, and be conscious that transformation will continuously happen. Some etiquettes are limited to specific organizations and they require to be complied with as well. While others, such as those listed in this section are mostly universal. Ultimately good business etiquette, like good business communication skills, requires good observation skills in order to learn what and how others are doing things, be it in your organization or other countries.

Written communication in business

"Writing, the art of communicating thoughts
to the mind through the eye, is the great
invention of the world"
-Abraham Lincoln

"Writing is easy. All you have to do is cross
out the wrong words"
-Mark Twain

Business Letters

A business person cannot afford the time and expense of personal visits to each and every one he transacts business with in different parts of the world, so he has to rely on written correspondence or phone calls. They are written to clients, prospective customers, managers, employees and business partners among others. Written correspondence helps him to keep in touch with clients and business associates and to preserve on paper, his or her conversation with them as a reference. The business letter acts as the paper representation of the business person and his organization, its appearance and presentation is vital to the image the client and business associates form of both the business person and the organization he or she represents. The common purposes of writing business letters are for:

1. **Sales efforts** – to introduce customers to new products and services.
2. **Relationship building** - to apprise or thank business associates or customers.
3. **Resolving an issue** – to resolve complaints that could involve a customer service issue, damaged product or even an inaccurate shipment.

4. **Selling incentive sales** - Selling incentive sales letters are used to offer rebates, coupons or special deals to long-term customers.
5. **Considerations** - a company may write a to a "lost customer" or someone who has not purchased products for a while.

Types of Business Letters

Business letters come in various forms. Depending on the recipient, they are written in varying tones, such as persuasive, informational, promotional or motivational tone. They have a clear purpose and objective, and they are targeted toward a specific individual or group.

Employees, management and other members of the business organization write various types of letters, these letters may be to ask for information, advice or favors, to send information, to collect money, to apologize, to sell, to apply for a job, etc. There are endless types of written letters, while some letters are easier to write than others, you cannot say one is more important than the others. The following are the most frequently written types of business letters:

1. **Sales Letters**: these letters include strong calls to action, detail the benefit to the reader of taking the action and include information to help the reader to act, such as including a telephone number or website link.
2. **Order Letters**: Order letters are sent by consumers or businesses to a manufacturer, retailer or wholesaler to order goods or services.
3. **Complaint Letters**: Are written to bring an issue to the attention of the company.
4. **Adjustment Letters**: An adjustment letter is normally sent in response to a claim or complaint.
5. **Inquiry Letters**: Inquiry letters ask a question or elicit information from the recipient.
6. Follow-Up Letter: Follow-up letters are usually sent after some type of initial communication.
7. **Letters of Recommendation**: Prospective employers often ask job applicants for letters of recommendation before they hire them.
8. **Acknowledgment Letters**: Acknowledgment letters act as simple receipts.

9. **Cover Letter**s: Cover letters usually accompany a package, report or other merchandise.
10. **Letters of Resignation**: Written when an employee plans to leave his or her job.

Standard and optional parts of a business letter

Business letters are usually divided into four main parts, each of these parts contain several essential and a few optional parts. The four parts are:
1. The heading
2. The opening
3. The body
4. The closing

The heading

The heading includes important parts like the letterhead, the date line and optional parts such as typed or printed headings and references.
1. **Letterhead** – Almost every company uses a quality printed stationary which states its name, address, telephone, fax, e-mail, website and other important information. Other details such as top executive and Board of Directors names and slogans are

optional. In addition to providing identification of the writers company, the content and design of the letter head help to project the company's image.

2. **Typed or printed heading** (optional) – When the organization does not have a letterhead, the address of the sender can be typed at the right hand corner of the page (or in the case where there is no stated address in the letterhead).

3. **Date line** – It is often very vital to know when the letter was written to both reader and writer, due to the fact that businesses receive a lot of letters every day, without the date it is almost impossible to recall the exact order of events relating to a particular matter. When it comes to dates, abbreviations of month and year are not recommended.

4. **Reference** (optional) – Some business letters contain references which are quoted by the person replying in order to help the mail staff when sorting and filing letters and the recipient know the exact sequence of the letters.

The opening

The aims of openings are to direct the letter to a specific person, company, department or section and to greet the reader. The inside address directs the letter and the attention line (if used). The salutation initiates mutual friendship.

1. **The inside Address** – The name and the address of the receiver which should always include a polite title (recommended), is usually the first lines of the inside address. The title of the addressee must be observed, such as Mr., Mrs., Miss. Ms., Dr., Prof., etc.

2. **Attention line** (optional) – When a letter is addressed to a company or department in a company, rather than addressing it to a specific person, an attention line is included below the inside address and above the salutation e.g. Attention: Human Resource manager.

3. **Salutation** – There are several forms of accepted salutations and each reflects a different tone, such as Dear Sir/Madam:, Dear Dr. John:, Dear John:, Your Excellency Sir:, etc.

The body

The body of the letter is definitely the most important section for both the reader and the writer. It is here that the writer makes every effort together his or her thoughts across to the reader effectively. The body of the letter consists of the message and may optionally include the subject line.

1. **The Subject line** (optional) – this line acts as a hint as to what the letter is all about; it is a quick identification of the topic of the letter.

2. **Message/body** – The message should be consisting of approximately two paragraphs and it should incorporate the earlier ideas, such as the 7c's and other elements of effective communication without compromising on the precision of the message and its correlation to the subject line.

The closing

Just as an individual says 'goodbye', when he/she has concluded a conversation, the same concept applies to a business letter's conclusion. The writer uses a complimentary ending, the only difference is the way he/she says it.

1. **Complimentary ending** – Complimentary endings, like salutations very in forms and tones; the important thing is to remember to match tone to that of the message as closely as possible e.g. cordially, yours sincerely, faithfully yours, etc.

2. **Company Signature** (Optional) – this is optional because some companies feel it is pointless to repeat information that always exists in the letterhead. It is the name and contact of the company, normally embossed on a stamp. It can also act as a way of validating the document's authenticity.

3. **Writers Signature** – this is simply the hand written signature of the writer, to validate the authenticity of the identity author or initiator of the message.

4. **Writers Identification and/or Designation** – in most cases the writers name, position and department are typed below his/her signature, this will give the letter more credibility in the nature of the authority the author possesses to communicate such a message.

5. **Reference Initials** – These are the typist's initials and the writer's in the cases were applicable. The writers initials should precede the typist in caps e.g. OKO/jno. If the writer is also the typist there is not need for the reference initials.

6. **Enclosures Notation** (optional) – When a document or other items are sent with the letter, the word Enclosure or Enclosures is typed below the reference initials.

7. **Carbon Copy Notation** (Optional)– this indicates the identity of the other people the writer has send the same copy of the letter to, e.g. CC: or C:
8. **Blind Carbon Copy Notation** (Optional) – this is an indication solely on the original document indicating the identity of all the other recipient of the same letter, e.g. BCC: or BC:
9. **Postscript** (Optional) – They are positioned at the end of the letter, but because it is part of the body of the letter it is typed in the same way as the main body e.g. PS: Bring this letter with you.

Business Letter Format

There are mainly two arrangement styles applicable to business letters and they are:

Block Format (also known as fully blocked), where all the elements are flushed to the left as illustrated to the right. All the elements of the letter except the letterhead are on the left side of the page. The company name and address; the recipient's name, title, company, and address; the letter's main text; the sender's typed name and title; and the attachment, enclosures, cc. are all single-spaced. Double-space or triple-space between the company's address and the date. Double-space or triple-space between the date and the recipient's name, between the recipient's address and salutation, and between the salutation and the letter's main text. Also double space or triple-space between the letter's main text and the closing (which is usually the word "sincerely"). Leave about four lines for the written signature, and double-space or triple-space between the title and the ending lines. The main text always single-spaced. Each paragraph is not indented but begins at the left margin. Double-space between the paragraphs.

Modified Block Format (also known as the Semi-Blocked), when most part of the letter is flushed to the left, except for the closing which is tabbed to the right as illustrated above. This letter type is slightly different from the first. The date, the closing, the signature, and title are all lined up along the center of the letter. They are not centered, but if you drew a line down the center of the letter, these elements would all be flush against this line. The main text is different, also. Single-space the text and indent the first sentence of each paragraph. Do not double-space between paragraphs. With both types of business letters, you may leave more space between each of the elements. With shorter letters you may wish to leave 3 blank lines between each element. You may also wish to drop the top margin down. The idea is to achieve good visual balance. Always try to keep a one-inch margin at the bottom and on the right and left sides. Never mix the block and modified block formats.

Other less popular formats but similar to the above stated include:

- ***The Modified-Block Format*** – With Indented Paragraphs: Paragraphs indented and double spaced
- ***Simplified Format*** – No salutation or complimentary closing, a subject line and a writer's identification are used.

In business, effective letters save on costs and even generate revenues, so it is vital that every letter written which is an investment of time, money and effort of the writer yield results.

Business Reports

Business reports provide vital information for management that is timely and factual. Business reports help to gathering important information and interpret the bulk of information in order to facilitate decision making. Various reports are carried out in thousands of modern businesses in order operate efficiently. In almost all positions ranging from management to public relations or accounts, report will be required, this is due to the fact that reports are used to monitor and control operations and they facilitated effective decision making.

A report by definition is an impartial objective planned presentation of fact to one or more individuals within or external to the organization for the purpose of conducting business. Normally, report carries more complex information than those in letters and memorandums. Many business are so large and complex that their operations is scattered throughout the city, nation and even international boundaries. In order for the business owner, manager or the head of department to get information on the business activities, he or she gets it through written report which is called business report. Reports vary due to the nature of information they carry.

A report is a presentation of facts, information and ideas. These presentation can be made periodically (daily, weekly, monthly or yearly) or they can occur just once in the organization as a special request. There are many types of report serving different purposes; some are analytical report, some are report of an experiment, others give the results of a survey investigation, while some tell the progress being made in the business or in a certain area of the business. Report may be sent from employees to management from the organizations to the stockholder, they can go to customers, supervisors and even to the staff. Memorandums may be used for report written for internal use in the organization, but longer report or report that go to top management and external people tends to be more formal in nature and is accompanied by a letter of transmission . The letter of transmission gives details on the purpose, scope of the report and acknowledgement of the sources of information that help in its

compilation. Business report can be classified according to the following;
1. Frequency - periodical or special
2. Origin - authorized or voluntary [accountability]
3. Function - to inform or to analyze
4. Subject - usually in keeping with the department of origin [financial report, performance report]
5. Formality - formal or informal in nature.
6. Type or appearance - letter form or memo form.

It should be noted that the above classification does not place report in to mutually exclusive categories, some report fall into several classes' e.g. Monthly authorized analytical reports in the form of a memo from the finance department. The purposes of reports can also vary extensively, but can fall more commonly into one of the following:
1. To assist management in running the organization
2. Report become permanent record and source of reference
3. Report can provide information to interested parties such as articles in the newspapers journals

4. Report help to identity, and recommend solutions to problems or issues in the organization

Types of Reports

On the basis of formality, reports can be two types:

- **Statutory reports:** are the ones required by law. Depending on the country and the laws, such reports are filed monthly, quarterly or annually and not filing them can bring about legal consequences.
- **Voluntary or non-statutory reports:** are not required by law, but most companies chose to keep them nonetheless. They are usually internal reports required by the management and are relevant to the company's well-being.

Reports can be of three main types depending on function:

- **Informative reports:** Report that give facts and other information on some aspects of the organization, such as sales report, performance report, bids submitted etc. These reports can be periodic or progressive in occurrence.
- **Analytical reports:** Reports that examine situations, problems, occurrences, draws

conclusions and makes recommendation along with the provision of data or/and information. These types of report can include justification reports, feasibility reports, and proposals.

- **Research reports:** These are reports based on research carried out by an external or internal team. They are created after the research has ended and they include conclusions, suggestions and other information originating from the researchers. These types of report are usually requested by the top management of the organizations.

Reports can also be categorized as formal and informal in nature. Informal business reports are normally communicated by email, memos, letters, or orally. While formal business report is usually submitted in print and may be the result of a series of reports. Common business reports include:

- Memo reports *(memoranda, memos)* are currently the most common means of exchanging written business information. Memos are short, informal messages that provide a rapid, convenient means of communication between employees within the same organization.

- A letter report is simply a report written in the form of a regular business letter. Unlike internal memo reports, which remain within the organization, letter reports are typically used for external communication. They may be used for personnel references, credit evaluations, or auditor recommendations.
- Agenda, minutes, and itineraries are common informational reports. Because they provide information without analysis or conclusions and recommendations, they are frequently written in semi-outline form. Also, because most organizations have standard formats for such reports, they are among the easiest to write.
- Expense reports are almost always printed forms because they are used on a regular basis and the same information is required each time for the organization's financial records.
- Personnel evaluations are used by Managers to routinely evaluate employees to provide them with feedback based on their job performance and to inform higher management of each person's abilities and promotability.
- A progress report is an informational report on the progress of a specific project. Most organizations use progress reports to track

the various projects underway at any given time. In small organizations, many project reports are delivered orally.

- Recommendation and justification reports present a problem and then provide the evidence required to justify a recommended solution to that problem. Unlike most reports, which are written at the request of management, recommendation and justification reports are often initiated by the writer, who has observed a problem and wishes to suggest a solution.
- Unlike other reports, proposals attempt to persuade. They may be either requested or volunteered, but they always propose to solve a problem for the reader, and they are written because the writer will benefit if the reader accepts the proposal.

Components of Business Reports.
As with other form of writing in organization the formats vary basing on the preference of it management and the influence of organizational culture. Most formal report generally contains the following parts.

1. **Introduction:** The introduction includes the background statement as to why the report was written, now the data was

gathered, what the report does not include the materials and equipments used. These information help the reader better evaluate the findings and conclusions of the report.

2. **Summary:** The summary is a brief presentation of the findings of the report and it is placed to facilitate busy executives who do not have the time to read the whole report. The summary helps the executives with quick decision making capabilities; the details can be read letter on.

3. **Body:** The body of the report contains the detailed presentation of the facts that has been gathered. The facts must be carefully assembled and neatly presented. The reader of the report depends solely on the writer's integrity.

4. **Conclusion and Recommendation:** The writer's conclusion tells the executive what the data gathered means and what he thinks should be done based on the findings. The nature of the report and the wishes of the person who requested it can determine where a recommendation is needed or not. Sometimes the

recommendations are rejected, adjusted or accepted and implemented.

It is important to note, that most formal reports are written in the third person; the readers of these reports are mainly interested in the third person; the readers of these reports are mainly interested in the information gathered. The closer the writer sticks to the facts the more objective he will report them, and the more valuable his report will be to those who make the final decisions. Quality typing and set up as with all forms at writings will increase the forcefulness of the communication by helping the reader rapidly absorb the key point. Longer and more formal reports usually consist of the following:
1. The cover
2. Title page
3. Letter of transmittal
4. Table of contents
5. Introduction
6. Summary (executive summary)
7. Body of the report
8. Conclusions and recommendations
9. Supplementary materials or appendix

Also included may be bibliography; special supplementary or complimentary materials like folders, photographs, books, maps, etc. A report must always be signed and should have the names and titles at those who compiled it either on their respective areas of contribution or at the end of the report.

Memorandums (Memo)

Memorandums can be used to request information, reinforce agreements, clarity prevision messages or acts as a short report. The memo is the equivalent of the business letter in internal communication and it represents about 50% of all written communication in organizations. Internal communication being all forms of communication that takes place within the organization. Memos are used to communicate with other employees of the same organization regardless of where the employee is located (same building or in a branch far away). It can be taken by hand via internal mail systems of an organization (network, fax) I can be delivered by hand to departments, pigeon holes or placed on a notice board in the organization.

Because the interoffice memo form has bees developed to save time, the formality of an inside address, salutation and complimentary closings are all omitted. The tone and manner that memos are written depends on the preference of the management of the company. Traditionally, memos tend to be formal and written in third person to avoid confusing facts and opinions. However, the trend is moving away from the rigid, formal writing styles of long ago. The tones of memos are memos are more recently influenced by the position of the writer in relation to the reader, but still the tone varies from organization to organization depending on their culture.

Benefits of memos

The memo is valuable for internal communication due to the following:

1. Carries a special formality and gets friendly reception (because both writer and reader belong to the same organization), this creates a cordial relationship amongst the two people.
2. Provides a written record of a message
3. Allows several individuals to receive the same message
4. Communications in all direction, upwards to managers, supervisors, executives to subordinates, laterally among people of equal rank, teams and departments required.

5. Reduces time and cost required to prepare communication.
6. Can use a variety of delivery systems including hands, fax and e-mail.

Purposes of memos

The main and most important reason for using memos as interoffice correspondence is to save on time. In business time is money, Memos are not as demand as letters and they enable the writer to just fours on the content. Memos are use for the identical reasons letters are used externally to the organizations. Memos fulfill the following purpose: Transmit information, Instruct, Announce, Congratulate, Express gratitude, Inform, Direct peoples, Request, Respond, and Confirm, to recommend and to persuade.

Many organizations have the policy of putting all important communications in writing , this will act as a record   , reference and is always filed , in this case the memo will act as the transmit all letters [transmittal memo]. Memos can be printed on plain paper using a standard format or template, or they may be written on preprinted forms. A good memo layout makes the massage appealing to the reader and allow quick of details. Memos are usually divided into three main parts:

Beginning: Introduction Purpose -The opening paragraph of a memo is important because it states the purpose of the memo, identifies the specific problems or project, provides backgrounds information and gives an overview of the information contained in the memo.

The opening of a memo must be reader focused due to the fact that it determines if the message will be reader or ignored. Using the altitude , positive tone will all make the memo readers attention; using convincing, positive tone will all make the memo readable to the reader by referring the reader to a previous communication (another memo, phone call, e-mail, fax or voice mail), a meeting or a topic of mutual interest.

Middle: Message/Discussion -The middle section is where the presentation of the message is made, in this section questions are answered, supporting information is provided and valid explanations are given for the purpose of the memo. The following should be achieved in the middle section of the memo:

1. The information meets the needs of the receiver.
2. The information answers or solves the problems identified.
3. The information incorporates the 7c's

Ending: Conclusion/Recommendation - The ending of the memo should be a separate paragraph that does one or more of the following:

- Restates the memo's purpose
- Highlights key information
- Summarizes the main points from the message
- Interprets the material presented
- Makes recommendations
- Suggest future action
- Express goodwill thoughts

The conclusion must correlate directly to the statement of purpose in the opening and should support the fact presented in the middle of the memo.

Listening: the least practiced aspect of communication

"Most people do not listen with the intent to understand; they listen with the intent to reply."
-Stephen R. Covey

"The most important thing in communication is hearing what isn't said."
-Peter Drucker

Listening Skills

Our ears are continuously assaulted by sounds every moment of the day. We hear these sounds, but don't listen to them; in self defense, we block off many sound from our consciousness. But too often we also block of sounds which we should be listening to, most people of acquired the bad habit of not listening even when they are with their best friends, relatives and in their work environment.

The main difference between hearing and listening is that listening involves the deliberate use of the mind to absorb the information. The key difference in the two is purpose, purpose being the reason as to listening or not listening. This purpose may be one of simple friendliness and sociability as in a party conversation; obtaining information as in a lecture or of critical analysis as in when observing a political debate; in all this scenarios listening intensity varies.

Listening is a fundamental communication skill which allows the receiver to understand both the verbal communication and the nonverbal content of the message. Listening is an active, not passive activity and it requires the listener

143

to be involved in the communication process. An active listener indicates both verbally and nonverbally that he or she is engaged in the conversation. When the speaker is communicating a feeling the listener can restate what the speaker is expressing by asking questions to reconfirm or clarify the message being received.

Also using nonverbal indicators of listening such as eye contact, head nodding, leaning forward, all can act as an encouragement for the speaker to continue. Lack of feedback from the listener can discourage the speaker from sharing opinions or feelings. By listening passively the listen may unintentionally short-circuit the conversation.

The different purposes of listening can imply different kinds of listening (active listening, passive listening or just hearing), but most good listening skills are basic to all kinds. Some basic rules are as follow; though they may sound similar they should all be observed to facilitate effective listening and ultimately good communication.

The Listening Model

All humans spend more time listening that talking, reading or writing. Business people spend roughly 70% of the working day communicating, half of that is spent listening, but only 25% of what is hear is retained. While people speak at 100 to 175 words per minute, but we can listen actively at up to 300 words per minute.

The model explains farther.

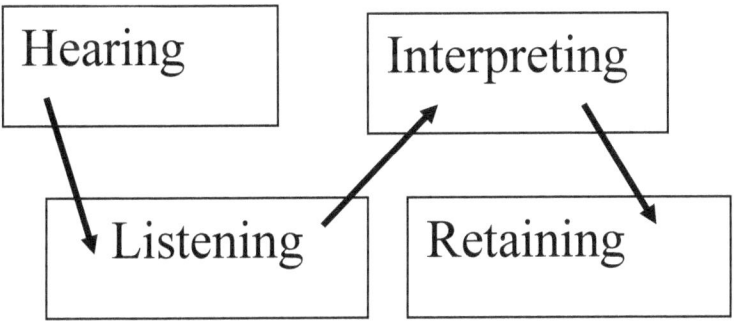

1. Hearing – the physical ability to perceive sound e.g. hearing nearby conversations or the humming of a computer without focusing on it or its meaning.
2. Listening – the act of filtering out distraction to allow understanding of the sounds e.g. when you ask a question you then listen for a response.

3. Interpreting – a mental function whereby the sound is analyzed to understand the meaning and then related to information and experience familiar to the listener.
4. Retaining – the act of remembering the interpreted sounds for future use.

Kinds of Listening

There are mainly to kinds of listening, active and passive listening. The difference between the two is found in the level of the listener's involvement.

- **Passive Listening** – the listener focuses at a minimal level and is able to absorb just enough of the speaker's words to stay involved in the speech or conversation. Passive listening is more appropriate if the listener is listening just for pleasure, in a case where it doesn't matter when the information is retained or not e.g. watching a movie or listening to music can induce passive listening.
- **Active Listening** – requires the listener to concentrate and focus in order to acquire the information being communicated, this is a requirement at the workplace and in school. Several of the information acquired in business settings requires retaining and this is only possible through active listening.

Overcoming Barriers to Listening

Being a good listener can make a difference between being a good manager and a mediocre one. Unfortunately, due to the fact that we were not taught to listen (unlike speaking) as children and the fact that nobody is born with good listening skills means being a good listener has to be a deliberate effort. It requires conscious practice to overcome the following barriers:

1. Not concentrating on what is being said
2. Becoming distracted by noise
3. Talking instead of listening
4. Having preconceived thoughts and opinions
5. Not being interested in what is being said

In order to encourage effective and good listening skills the following should be observed:

- **Get ready to listen** – good listening requires a readiness to listen with an understanding as to why you are going to listen and what you should be listening for. This requires that you prepare yourself physically, mentally, and emotionally. Practically turning your back on distractions and seating close enough to see and hear what the speaker is saying.

- **Accept your share of responsibility** – very often listeners approach a speaker with a "show me" attitude; he or she dares the speaker to interest him/her in the communication. This kind of attitude is discourteous and tough on the speaker. The sooner it is recognized that listening is a shared responsibility in communication the sooner good listeners will be made. The quality of courtesy and listening can affect the talking of the speaker and even in some cases it can control it.
- **Listen with understanding** – be certain that you understand the speakers ideas fully and completely, don't jump to conclusions about false or half-true statements. This means your must listen carefully and ask question if necessary to clarify anything that is vague or ambiguous.
- **Listen with an open mind** – Keep your mind open when listening, forget your biases and prejudices for the moment and be ready to receive new ideas. Don't refuse to listen to new ideas just because it conflicts with those you are familiar with.
- **Listen actively** – Listening actively basically means three things on your part: concentration, relating what you hear to what you already know, and reading

between the lines to sense implied meanings.

- **Listening with empathy** – listening with empathy means putting yourself in the speaker's place so as to see through his/her eyes, naturally such listening requires imagination. Empathic listening help dispel any shyness, suspicion or hostility on the speakers part. Listening with empathy helps effective communication and yields great rewards.

Listening is an invaluable skill for managers to use on a daily basis on the job. By actively listening the manager show empathy for and understanding of the speakers even if from a different position to the manager's own position. This is important when managers negotiate with each other or with customers. Employees and other managers are unlikely to bring problems a manager who has poor listening skills, which in turn can undermine a manager's credibility and limits his/her effectiveness.

Bibliography

Baxter, Leslie A., and Dawn O. Braithwaite, eds. 2008. Engaging theories in interpersonal communication: Multiple perspectives. Thousand Oaks, CA: SAGE.

Boone, LE & Kurtz, DL (2010) "Contemporary Business" NY: John Wiley & Sons

Brounstein, M., Bell, A.H., Smith, D.M., Isbell, C & Orr, A. (2010) "Business Communication" NY: John Wiley & Sons

Canary, Daniel J., Michael J. Cody, and Valerie L. Manusov. (2008). Interpersonal communication: A goals-based approach. 4th ed. Boston: Bedford/St. Martin's.

Coiro, Julie and others, Eds. Handbook of Research on New Literacies. NY: Lawrence Erlbaum Associates, 2008.

DeVito, John A. 2009. The interpersonal communication book. 12th ed. Boston: Allyn & Bacon.

Eunson, B. (2012) "Communication in the Workplace" NY: John Wiley & Sons

Galvin, KM (2010). Making connections: Readings in relational communication. 5th ed. Oxford: Oxford Univ. Press.

Guffey, M. E. & Loewy, D (2012). Essentials of Business Communication, 9th Ed. Southwestern Cengage Learning

Guffey, M.E. & Almonte, R. (2010) "Essentials of Business Communication" CT: Cengage Learning

Guffey, M.E., Rhodes, K., Rogin, P. & Rhodes, K. (2009) "Business Communication: Process and Product" CT: Cengage Learning

Heiner, M. (2005) 'Challenges of teamwork in production: demands of communication', Organization Studies, vol. 27, no. 1, pp. 103–24.

Jain, A. K. (2001). Professional Communication Skills. New Delhi: S. Chand & Company Limited.

Kupritz, V. W.& Cowell, E. (2011, January). Productive management communication: Online and face-to-face. Journal of Business Communication, 48(1), 70–71.

Lehman, C & DuFrene, D. (2010) Business communication

Locker, KO (2006). Business and administrative communication (7th ed.). New York: McGraw-Hill Irwin.

Margaret, C. (2000). A Guide to Effective Writing. Kuala Lumpur: Prentice Hall.

Newman, A & Ober, A. (2012). Business Communication: In Person, In Print, Online. CT: South-Western Cengage Learning

Nielsen, J. (2008). Effective Communication Skills: The Foundations for Change

Ober, S. (2007). Fundamentals of contemporary business communication (2nd ed.). New York: Houghton Mifflin.

Samovar, L.A., Porter, R.E. & McDaniel, E.R. (2011). "Intercultural Communication: A Reader" CT: Cengage Learning

Thill, J. V., & Bovée, C. L. (2007). Excellence in business communication (7th ed.). Upper Saddle River, NJ: Pearson Prentice Hall.

Verderber, K., Verderber, R. & Berryman-Fink, C. (2007). Interact: Interpersonal communication concepts, skills, and contexts. (11th ed.). New York: Oxford University Press.

Wilson, G L (2001) Groups in context: leadership and participation in small groups, 6th edn, McGraw-Hill, New York.

Wood, J. (2010). Interpersonal communication: Everyday encounters, 6th ed. Boston: Wadsworth.

Camp, SC & Satterwhite, ML (2006). College English and Communication,

www.ingramcontent.com/pod-product-compliance
Lightning Source LLC
Chambersburg PA
CBHW051215170526
45166CB00005B/1903